Where is tomorrow?

Where is tomorrow?

Rev. Eliza Armstrong

First published in 2013 as a Kindle edition

Library of Congress Control Number:		2016911581
ISBN:	Hardcover	978-1-5245-9313-1
	Softcover	978-1-5245-9312-4
	eBook	978-1-5245-9311-7

Print information available on the last page.

Rev. date: 07/19/2016

To order additional copies of this book, contact:
Xlibris
800-056-3182
www.Xlibrispublishing.co.uk
Orders@Xlibrispublishing.co.uk
742527

CONTENTS

SECTION 2

The Humanist Attitude to Death

I dedicate this book to my dear Husband Ron who has loved and cared for me endlessly over 58 years. Without his patience and encouragement I would have not managed to write this book. Ron is a quiet, gifted Christian Man and I thank God for him every day.

I am indebted to all my family especially my eldest grandson Jonathan Philips (who helped me with the computer), without whom I just would not have gone on.

My husband Ron has been of great encouragement. He has been patiently doing other things (things that I should have been doing) so that I might have the time to study.

PREFACE

The question – if not often asked and certainly often pondered in the human heart and mind – 'Is there life after death?' has its own poignancy. It is something we would all like to believe as being true. If there is truly life after death, then we would all meet our loved ones who have long since passed on and so there would be instant comfort for mourners and assurance that this life is not all that there is. So do we live in vain? We often long for proof of immortality; however, life after death is not verifiable, only falsifiable, since not one person who is accepted by all the faith has ever witnessed to the fact.

The question of 'Human existence after death?' has been the subject of many philosophers in past centuries, and will provide a point of discussion in the future. It is hoped that this book will not only give an historical account of philosophies on immortality but will also show that it is a belief that (a) affects our present life, (b) is reasonable to the human intellect, and (c) is inseparably rooted in Christian hope. In presenting some arguments, we may seem to be moving towards an argument for theism. This is not the point of this book, although in presenting some aspects – that is, the connection between morality and immortality – this work seems to be moving towards that end. All the historical arguments for life after death cannot be presented in this small work, except some of them. No distinction will be made between the terms 'life after death', 'immortality', and 'eternal life'. These expressions will simply be used synonymously.

We begin from the standpoint of a Christian theist who believes that there is only one God, and His very being is goodness and love. These attributes cannot be separated from the fact that God exists since they are His nature. Christians believe that the goodness and love of God are revealed in His Son Jesus Christ, the Incarnate Lord. Christians also believe that in the humanity of Christ we have revealed to us human nature as God intends it to be. In Christ, an 'ensign' is held before us of perfect obedience to God and, 'as the next paragraph will show', to the moral law. In Christ only we see the perfect personality towards which we must strive asymptotically but which we never completely gain in this life.

The Torah was given to Moses when God revealed Himself to the prophet; the Law is therefore not only God's will but also a reflection of His nature. 'You shall be holy for I am holy'. The command is categorical, man's chief end to glorify God and to imitate His divine nature. The command is also given by Christ: 'You must be perfect even as your Father in heaven is perfect.' When we state the chief end of man and the categorical command, we give rise to two questions: How can an infinite being ever hope to be perfect? How can a finite being ever hope to imitate the divine nature? In order to attempt an answer to these questions, it is good to discuss topics such as attitudes to death, what a person is, arguments for immortality, and the problem of evil. Finally, we hope to show how these arguments are greatly strengthened by the postulation of Christian Revelation.

Although this book is written from the standpoint of Christian faith, it is to be remembered that human beings are not immortal by nature; only God is by nature immortal. Immortality is not the central emphasis of the Christian faith; the triune God recognised as Father, Son, and Holy Spirit is the undisputed centrality of faith. Remembering this, it is to be understood that immortality must be a gift that is bestowed upon mankind by his Creator, just as this life and all that we have that we believe to be a gift by the grace of God through Jesus Christ His Son.

Life after death is bound up in the self-giving of God. The Christian belief in God as a benevolent Father, the moral conscience, and life after death are interrelated. God's will, as shown in the Torah, is adhered to through the morality or lack of it practised by individuals in this life.

As Christians, we believe that this life has value, so it must be respected at all stages of development, since it is seen as a time of preparation or 'soul-building'; thus our moral actions are inseparable from our hope of life after death. Yet a mere existence, even an eternal existence where there was no 'self' or personal survival, would (in the minds of most people) be no better than the thought of total annihilation. So the life to come has value in Christian belief. 'Afterlife' existence is personal and well worth all the heartaches and moral effort of this life.

'It is the quality of life for which a man believes himself. To be made that makes all the difference; there is nothing. Inspiring in the mere thought that one is destined to go on living, in the bare sense of being alive, for an indefinitely long period.'[1]

Of course, it is not in the Christian faith alone that belief in life after death is found. In ancient Egypt, in the Vedic faith of India and

---

[1] A.E. Taylor, 'The Christian Hope of Immortality'.

in Islam, there is a belief in judgement according to actions lived or not in this life, and of reward and punishment in the next life. However, in order to make it clear that belief in the moral nature of God, the value of this life and the next has not been 'evidenced' with primitive man. The Israelite and Greek concept of life after death is well worth mentioning in order to make it clear that belief in the moral nature of God, the value of this life and the next life, and belief in the moral nature of God when compared with primitive thought is an innovation and a real preparation for the Christian concept of life after death.

CHAPTER 1

A Very Short History of Belief in Life after Death

In all the animal kingdom, man is unique in his concept of death; he knows that he is going to die, but he does not know when. He does not believe that death is the end of living; there is another mode of living to come. Man is the only animal to inter his dead, and it is from the graves of primitive man that we learn that belief in some kind of existence was held as long as half a million years ago.

The Neanderthal man placed food and implements of flint in the graves of the dead some 10,000 to 25,000 years ago. The Old Stone Age man, the Co-magnums who roamed southern Europe and Africa around 25,000 to 10,000 years ago, the hunters of game, buried ornaments, food, and weapons in the graves of their dead. In the New Stone Age, around 10,000 to 5,000 years ago, the Neolithic man adopted even more elaborate funeral arrangements, the deceased often being placed in the foetal position. Was this an expectation of another birth? It could well be so.

If we look at the studies made before the First World War of surviving primitive people in Australia, Polynesia, Africa, and

South America, we find that further evidence was found of a very primitive belief in life after death. Sir James Fraser summarises the results of his enquiry into primitive eschatology.

'It is impossible not to be struck by the strength, and perhaps we may say the universality, of the natural belief in immortality among the savage races of mankind. With them a life after death is not a speculation and conjecture of hope and fear, it is a practical certainty which the individual as little dreams of doubting as he doubts the reality of his conscious existence. He assumes it without inquiry and acts upon it without hesitation, as if it were one of the best ascertained truths within the limit of human experience.'[2][3][4][5]Sir James Fraser. see next page.

In primitive eschatology, however, there are no hopes for a valuable immortality among the savage races of mankind; life beyond the grave was thought of as a shadowy replica of this life. There is every reason to suppose that in early times the Greeks accepted much the same 'picture' of the 'hereafter' as other more primitive peoples. According to Homer, man possesses a psyche along with his bodily 'selfhood'. The psyche is a shadowy double or ghost of man's bodily self. For most people, the afterlife was spent in a dark underworld, but a few outstanding individuals, heroes and demigods, are 'transported' to the Elysian Fields 'intact', without actually going down to death at all, or having their souls separated from their bodies. But for the majority, Hades is the destiny of all who die.

---

[2]

[3]

[4]

[5] Sir James Fraser – 'Belief in Immortality and the Worship of the Dead' (vol.1, p. 468).

When in the eleventh book of the Odyssey, Odysseus tries to comfort the dead Achilles by suggesting that he was such a mighty man when he walked this earth that he may be powerful among the dead, Achilles answers, 'Don't speak to me of death: I would sooner be a hireling servant of the most penurious man alive than the ruler over all the kingdoms of the dead.'

Early in the history of Israel we read in the Old Testament that Yahweh (God) was concerned with the community. Justice was social rather than personal. The dead went to the dark underworld of Sheol. Yahweh was God of the living. A few isolated individuals like Enoch were 'lifted up to the heavens', but there was no promise of personal immortality; for the good man, the reward would be many descendants.

A new deeper understanding of Yahweh was expounded by the prophets of the seventh and sixth centuries. Jeremiah was the first to formulate the idea of individual as well as corporate moral responsibility (Jer. 31:30f): 'But everyone shall die for his own sins. Each man who eats sour grapes, his teeth shall be set on edge.' At this time, there were developments along the same line in Iran in the teachings of Zoroaster.

With the Babylonian conquest of Judah, the fall of Jerusalem, and the exile of her political and religious leaders, national confidence was shaken. She no longer had her rituals, her temple, or her feasts. God's chosen people were no longer a 'tight-knit' community in their own land, which Yahweh had given them. The individual began to think of his own personal destiny and his own relationship with Yahweh. We see God's justice towards the individual in the book of Job. But it was probably during the struggles and martyrdom of the Maccabeus revolts that a belief, possibly arising from Zoroastrianism, in the resurrection of the dead formulated.

The prophets of Israel had held her to a strict monotheism; there were no thoughts of 'gods' of the dead. The old beliefs in ghosts had been wiped out, and the way was now open for a more spiritual interpretation of man's relationship to God. The belief in a future resurrection of the righteous to a better life grew within the socio/religious party of the Pharisees in post-exilic Israel. First, it is worth noting that among these post-exilic Pharisees' resurrection was not thought of as in Greek philosophy, where it was believed that at death there was an escape of the soul from the prison of the body but as a resurrection of the whole body, a concept adopted into Christianity: 'I believe in the resurrection of the flesh' (The Apostles' Creed). Secondly, this was a belief of the ordinary people, the belief was very much linked with their conduct in the here-and-now, and an individual's final destiny was to be established by God alone who is King. The judgement would be good because it would be made by Yahweh who is Holy, the Highest Wisdom, and Creator of all things.

The belief in a good life after death came into Greek thought through the mystery cults – the Elysian, Dionysian, and Orphic mysteries. Firstly, personal immortality was the focal point. Secondly, the initiate was promised a life of bliss in the hereafter, which the non-believers was denied. However, the real preparation for belief in personal immortality based upon the actions in this life and afterlife as a better life in the Gentile world was due primarily to Platonic philosophy. Plato dismisses the idea of ghosts; he is emphatic on the matter of the quality of immortality, which he teaches. It is a life that centres its interest on things that are unseen and as such often disregarded, things such as truth, beauty, and goodness. But Plato is weak where the Israelite is strong; his immortality is one in which the body has no share; it is an immortality of the soul only, which is god-like in nature and thus can survive death. In Plato, there is no direct dependence of the hope of eternal life on the moral character of God; Plato justified his assurance of immortality not on the consideration of the Nature of God but on the inherent nature of the soul. God, according to Plato, has ordered the world so that if man lives rightly, he will gain 'salvation', but there is no grace, no free gift of God to help man live rightly and so gain 'salvation'. God will not intervene to help man with his struggles.

It was Christianity that integrated, in the one concept, the thoughts of a new higher quality of eternal life, and of God as the only source and guarantee of survival of the whole man to eternal life.

CHAPTER 2

Morality and Immortality

Starting from the belief that there is only one God whose being or nature is love and goodness, attributes which cannot be separated from Him because they are part of His nature, Christians believe that the love and goodness of God are fully revealed in Jesus Christ. The command given by Jesus – 'Be ye perfect even as your Father in Heaven is perfect' – along with the fact that Christians believe that man's chief end is to glorify God or reflect the image of God raises two questions. Firstly, how can a finite person ever hope to be perfect as God is perfect? Secondly, how can a person, who is finite, ever glorify or reflect the image of God who is infinite?

When arguing from morality to immortality, it is important to note that 'immortality' or life after death is not the central emphasis of the Christian faith; it is a gift that proceeds from God the Father through Jesus Christ His Son. The life we now live is also a gift from God. For the Christian, 'life after death' is bound up in the self-giving love of God in Jesus Christ His Son. In this book, it is important to show how Christian belief in God as a loving Father who in Himself is goodness and love, and with this in mind we can understand how the moral conscience and life after death are truly inter-related.

Christianity admits a natural law of morality, which is available to non-Christians. Saint Paul asserts that 'Gentiles . . . show that what the law requires is written on their hearts'. However, this natural law may not be identical in every society. For instance, in primitive society monogamy may not be accepted as in Western Christendom, but the basic law that a caring long-term relationship is best would be acceptable to both societies.

Morality is bound up in the concepts of good and bad – right and wrong. We state, for example, that it is wrong to kill and that it is good to love one's neighbour; people who accept the objectivity of morality believe that when an action is praised because it is morally good or condemned because it is morally bad, a value judgement of some kind is being made. Thus, to state that it is wrong to maltreat a child is to make a statement that condemns the action because of the value of the child as a human being. Similarly, if we say it is good to help a blind man across the road, we assert that that action is good because of the value of the blind man as a human being. These kinds of statements are also made with reference to animals. So we conclude from all this that we care and respect living persons and animals simply because in them there is life; we state the value of life as life, not be used as a mere means to an end.

H. P. Owen writes that moral values affect us in the following two ways: 'Firstly, they attract us towards moral ideals to which we aspire. But we all experience conflict, we all feel that we want to do that which is morally good and at the same time feel drawn towards that which is morally bad.' In his book called *The Existence of God* (chapter 9), Swinburne points out that this element of limited free choice in moral actions is compatible with beings of limited free will, since a being has free will only if his intentional actions are not fully determined. The limitation of free will being that if the choice of good or bad is up to him, then he must comprehend in some way what is morally good even if inclined to do what is morally bad. Swinburne believes the limited choice of freedom leaves man free to 'move towards the Divine or to return to the level of the beast' (p. 159). Moral insight is given to human beings only. The goal to be aimed at is the cultivation of moral goodness or, as St Augustine states, 'to desire to do the will of God'. This aspiration to goodness aims to overcome the desires that we feel towards the morally bad.

Secondly, moral values according to Owen can be analysed in terms of obligation. People are not only attracted to values that are good; we also feel obligated to exercise these values. Owen illustrates the difference between these two effects: 'attraction and obligation'.

Let us suppose we are contemplating someone who is conspicuously good. In so far as we are attracted to him, we may say, 'How I wish I were like that!' But in so far as he presents a challenge, we say, 'How I ought to be like that!'

Moral values are not only ideals that attract us but also facts that impose unconditional obligation.

The fact that we aspire to moral goodness does not prove the existence of that goodness, since we could just as easily aspire to a mere 'whim', something quite meaningless. A 'whim' can be irrational, phobic, or compulsive. For instance, I may suddenly decide, for no good reason, that my house should be painted red throughout, and although I may feel strongly about painting my house red inside and outside, in no way would I feel obligated to do so; I would feel no obligation either to hold that particular 'whim' or to carry it into action. On the other hand, goodness places us under obligation and under constraint; if we feel that an action is morally bad, we feel constrained from committing that action. For instance, in marriage, a person may want to be disloyal to their partner, but the lack of goodness in such disloyalty would constrain that person to desist from the act. It could be argued that it is a lack of goodness in such an action to constrain him/her from this action. That can become more realistic when we realise that goodness and love are held together in the nature of God, just as they are held together in marriage and with all our relationships with other people. The love mentioned above is agape, described as an awareness of the value and response to the value of persons.

H. P. Owen questions whether this goodness or, more correctly, this absolute goodness is personal or impersonal.

'Are we to equate it with Plato's idea of the good or with the personal God of Christianity?'[6]

In this life, in this world, moral ideals are found in persons and not in things, so how can a person participate in or even hope to reflect a goodness that is impersonal? Plato's forms can attract; they do not impose obligation; whereas moral values, because of their nature, put us under obligation whether we respond to these values or not. For instance, a person may break a promise to visit a friend. He/she might break the promise and have very good reasons for doing so, but that person would still feel obligated to that first promise and would apologise and try to make amends. We do not only reject goodness in itself, how can we ever feel in debt to Platonic forms, or feel guilty when we fail to respond to them? We could not betray values if they were impersonal. I believe that Owen speaks the truth when he says, 'Personal theism gives the only explanation that value claims in here in the character and will

6

of God'. . . . If we accept this position, then the logical conclusion to reach is that when we reject value claims or the 'pull' towards good, we do not only reject goodness in itself but the goodness and love that God is in His nature.

We can sum up all of this as follows:

(a) The natural law or awareness of moral good and bad flows from the eternal love and goodness of God. It is not necessary to know God in order to be aware of moral goodness. Ontologically, morality is dependent on God, but epistemologically morality is autonomous.
(b) The 'attractive' and obligatory nature of moral values is well suited to our creaturely existence. Swinburne states that it is reasonable that God made persons with bodies, since an agent has a body, which is the part of the world through which his intentions are executed and through which he inspires (p. 160). The knowledge referred to here is of the laws of nature, expected states of the world, and the effects one person can produce by their actions in the world (p. 198).
(c) Swinburne also states, 'If we were perfectly good, we would we would not feel obligated to do what it good, so would not feel the "pull" towards good since we would no inclinations towards bad.' Such singleness or goodness, which would be required to free us from the moral law, can never be attained in this life, yet that perfect state of being is that for which the Christian strives.

Our ultimate aim in performing morally good deeds is to express in our creaturely existence the goodness of the Creator. This life is a time of preparation or soul-building for the time when the Christian is able to reflect the goodness of God in the life after death. On this view, morality demands eternal life as mankind's final goal. But how does the atheist fit into all of this? Surely atheists have a moral conscience too?

John Hicks attempts an answer to the above question in his book *The existence of God.* He tells a parable of a Christian and an atheist; both journey through this life, each apparently making the same journey. But for the atheist, this life is all there is; therefore, any choice he makes between good and bad will be determined by what he considers to be good for humanity in this life only, and he believes that the moral conscience of man has been cultivated by the evolution of society and by the needs of society. The atheist would state that he does look beyond this life in a way because the good and bad actions he performs will influence the lives of future generations when he is dead. For the atheist, the journey along the road of this life leads nowhere.

The Christian also believes that he has a duty towards society and that his actions will influence future generations, but for him the 'pull' towards what is good and the realisation of what is bad or wrong are both God-given gifts to help him in this soul-building journey towards 'the Celestial City'.

Christians and atheists do not have different experiences along the road; both experience emotional and physical joys and sorrows. Both have the same expectations about what life will entail, but the goal is different, and the trials of life are viewed differently. The Christian's realisation of good and bad, right and wrong is realised through Christian revelation that 'deepens the insight that nature itself affords' (Owen, p. 118). What a man knows by nature is fully revealed and perfected by Jesus Christ; not only the nature of morality is revealed but the way in which we experience forgiveness resolves our feelings of guilt over our transgressions of the natural law i, possible only through the death of Jesus Christ on Calvary. In His life of obedient self-sacrifice, Jesus embodies the goodness and love of God. We are challenged to be like Him: 'Be ye perfect even as your Father in Heaven is perfect.' We are attracted to the value claims that are embodied in Him, and we are placed under obligation by their challenge.

When we think of the obligation, such actions as promise-keeping, truth telling, love of one's neighbour, those are all actions for which utilitarian justification can be given. Such actions are obligatory if they add to the perfection, or lead nearer to the perfection of this universe, what Kant calls the 'summum bonum'. The moral strivings of Christians are made in response to the revelation of the will of God in Jesus Christ. God's will towards us and for us is goodness and love.

Goodness and love in mankind leads to happiness. The best known argument from happiness to God and immortality is the Kantian one. However, other philosophers have put forward different forms of the same argument. The happiness referred to in these arguments is not a hedonistic pleasure but a spiritual happiness that may be defined as a good moral conscience.

Owen states (p. 91, chapter 5), 'The pursuit of happiness, no less than the responses to moral claims, also requires the postulation of eternal life.'

When that definition of happiness is given, then the response to moral values and happiness are inter-related in the Christian pilgrimage towards his chief end. This happiness cannot be attained without moral response, and moral response leads to this happiness since happiness involves having an experience of actions and so forth. Which cause a person to feel 'the pleasure of a good conscience'.[7] This does not mean that all morally good actions are executed only in the pursuit of happiness. We are not continually aware that we are seeking happiness.

'A man need not be always preoccupied with the end of his journey with every step he takes' (Aquinas). Many good acts are performed out of compassion, love, or sympathy, but as Aquinas so beautifully states, 'None can reach happiness without good will and the loves of one who sees God inevitably fall in with the Divine Plan.'

Man cannot have complete happiness of this spiritual kind in this life, since to have such, he would have to be perfectly sinless, which no man is. Another life, a life after death, is necessary for man to realise this happiness in full. As stated earlier, God as He is revealed in Jesus Christ is the centre from which all things flow, including life after death. If absolute goodness is to be taken as man's chief end, it is very easy to see that the chief end cannot be reached in this life. Even the outward claims of morality cannot be satisfied in this life; the inner claims which are claims on our purity of heart and will are a more clear indication of how far we fall short of perfection.

Yet our final end is not only that which we desire; we are not only attracted towards it; we are also under obligation to strive to reach it. For man to reach his goal, there must be something beyond this life; there must be another existence in life after death – a different but conscious mode if existence in which man may realise true happiness as defined above, and where, like looking through a mirror, he will reflect the full image of the goodness and love, which is God. Man can only and will 'reflect' that goodness, since the Creator remains the Creator for all eternity and man

---

7

remains creature; so man will not ever be that goodness; he can only be a reflection of that which is perfect. To use Swinburne's symbolism . . ., we may conclude that the possibility (p) of the hypotheses (h) that there is life after death, given the evidence (e) that Jesus has revealed the goodness and love of God to us, plus the background knowledge of man's moral conscious (k) is much higher than p (h/e).

CHAPTER 3

The Argument against Immortality from the Fact of Death

One of the most obvious and universal arguments against immortality is the fact of death itself. Put very simply, the argument is thus stated: How can we, as intelligent, perceptual beings believe in a life which is not destroyed by the dissolution of the body? It is certain that we all die, and there is no evidence that with death a person is not completely annihilated. This argument is clearly worthless since it only states that which no intelligent person, Christian or otherwise, will deny – namely, that death is inevitable and that man's existence as an animate, intelligent being ceases at death, to be observable by observers. We can no longer hear (after the burial) or see the deceased. We cease to be influenced by his actions. In other words, the man, at death, ceases to be an object of our sense perception.

Against this, it must be pointed out that very often our senses deceive us; therefore, we cannot argue simply from the point of sense perception. For instance, if the weather is very cold outside, thereby making us feel very cold, the water in the swimming pool will feel warm. But if it is hot outside and we feel very hot, that same swimming pool will feel cold. Our senses can deceive us in many ways. To use Kant's illustration of pink spectacles, if we were wearing pink-tinted spectacles, everything within our scope of vision would appear to be pink in colour, and we all know that grass, trees, and rivers are not pink. It is not only our tactile and visual senses that can be deceived . . . It is a well-known fact that sound, which exceeds eighty decibels, cannot be heard by the human auditory organs. Yet that sound exists as sound and can be heard by many different animals.

We are confined by the limits of our temporal existence; most intelligent people will admit that temporal existence has limits, although our limits are decreasing as humanity progresses. We need only think of the science of microbiology to realise that what was once thought of as either an invasion by satanic forces or a God-inflicted punishment for sins committed is really an invasion of harmful organisms that cause disease to the body. As Ian Crombie pointed out that we cannot see the 'whole picture', our vision is limited by the time, location, and the extent of our knowledge at the moment of any experience of perception.

This argument can be carried further. The experience of the mystic is not observable to us using our sense perception, but obviously he is having a meaningful experience. Sometime in the future, the mystic may find a language to describe what he experiences in terms both understandable to others and truly appropriate to his experience, and so we know there is a possibility that some way of perceiving what the mystic experiences may be found. To use Queen Victoria by way of analogy, if someone had told Her (Late) Majesty that one day a man would walk on the moon, touching it, hearing the sounds of it, and seeing its surface at his feet, I doubt if she would have believed it or even thought it possible in her wildest imaginings. So we know it is never safe to declare that anything that we cannot experience by means of sense perception at a particular moment in time is simply nothingness or logically impossible. In my own lifetime, television, mobile phones, computers, and many other things have been created from human intelligence.

When we come to ask whether we can believe that a life is not destroyed by the dissolution of the body, we find that this part of the argument is also weak. What we can believe, or are capable of believing, depends upon our geographical, historical, and cultural placing in the temporal world. The historical dependence is illustrated on the analogy of Queen Victoria. Geographical and cultural dependence often go together. If we lived in India and were of the Hindu faith, we would find no difficulty in believing that we would someday be reincarnated in the form of some living animal.

If we were among the starving masses of this world, we would think 'three square meals' a day to be unliveable bliss; whereas here in our Western society, these three means are accepted as one of the facts of our everyday existence.

We have no means of verifying or falsifying that death is the absolute annihilation of a human being. A person exists in this life, and A. E. Taylor points out that that the word 'existence' when applied to a person has a double sense; it may mean existence as one object among others, observable by others as part of their environment. But it may also mean existence as a subject aware of self, and it is not self-evident that these two senses of 'existence' must always go together. We cannot say, for instance, that we can be aware of self without also being aware of objects that are not self. Yet on the other hand, we are often aware of self – our own well-being – or otherwise without seeming to be aware of anything else. We can be equally aware of self without anyone else being aware of us – for instance, in the darkness of a cinema of the 'loneliness' of a crowded room.

Although we have seen other people die, we ourselves have never been the subject of death; we can only look at death objectively until we ourselves die. We have no right to say that a person who ceases to exist objectively also ceases to exist subjectively, as a subject of experience and existence. We have never experienced death, so how then can we explain the experience of dying? Can we truly speak of dying ever being experienced at all? If dying means not only to cease to exist as the experience of someone's observation but also to cease to exist as a subject who experiences, then the experience of dying would simply be a transition from experiencing to having no experience, of feeling to having no feeling. But it is a contradiction in terms to speak of experiencing a lack of experience or feeling a lack of feeling. Yet unless both conditions are experienced, it is meaningless to talk about the experience of dying. It seems then that dying as merely a cessation of existence as an experiencing subject must be an event that no creature can experience, just as none can experience coming into being in the sense of a transition from being nothing at all to being something. Both these events, therefore, must be events in their own nature that can never be experienced by anyone but only observed by those who are not involved in the events. Such observation cannot be conclusive, since it depends on the accuracy of the observer and his capability of description. The observer can satisfy himself that something that the observable is now unobservable . . . But he cannot observe existence passing into non-existence or vice versa. These two transitions are as incapable of being observed as they are of being experienced. A. E. Taylor states,

> The reason that they are incapable of being observed is not simple that like physical events which can be asserted to take place in the sub-microscopic world, they are on too small a scale of us to detect them, or that, in some other way the physical conditions necessary for the stimulations of our sense organs are not fulfilled; it is that it is a formal logical absurdity to think of a condition of non-existence at all; there is no such a condition, and therefore there can be no transition from it to anything else or from anything else to it.[8]

'The coming to be of something before wholly non-existent would be no transformation, but absolute origin, and the sheer ceasing of anything to exist would be annihilation.'

The reason for why death occurs is approached by different groups of people and different individuals in various ways. The account of death accepted by a group or an individual will greatly influence their belief or lack of belief in life after death. For this reason, we will compare the humanist and the Christian attitudes to death.

---

8 A.E. Taylor, 'The Christian Hope of Immortality'.

SECTION 2

The Humanist Attitude to Death[9]

There are various humanist approaches to death – the emotional, the theoretical, and the biological being three examples of the approaches. The biological would probably be the most widely expounded and accepted approach. From this point of view, death is seen as a necessary part of the process of evolution. The argument usually states that if death did not occur, and new members of the race kept being born, then the world would soon become overcrowded. Humanists have also maintained that it is the differences between individuals and generations that have made improvements in the race possible.[10][1] F. A. Crew in *The Humanist Outlook* points out that the habitats of humans and lower animals undergo continuous change. According to Crew, it is fact that a species is in harmony with its environment and is able to adapt to change that determines the survival of species.

9

10

Crew goes on to argue that if conditions in this earth had been completely stable, socially and environmentally, then there would be no real need for the capacity to adjust and change.

'There came into being a system of replacement. The old, inefficient in respect to the abilities to reproduce and to adapt, are removed by natural death and replaced by the young, efficient in reproduction and adaptability.'[11][12]

Bertrand Russell in *Mysticism and Logic* sums up the humanist attitude to death in the following way:

> That man is the product of causes which had no prevision of the end they were achieving; that his origins, his growth, his hopes and fears, his loves and his beliefs are but the outcome of accidental collocations of atoms; that no fire, no heroism, no intensity of thought or feelings can ever preserve an individual life beyond the grave; that all the labours of all the ages, all the devotion, all the inspiration, all the noonday brightness of human genius are destined to extinction in the vast death of the solar system, and that the whole temple of mans' achievement must inevitably be buried beneath a debris of a universe in ruin – all these things, if not quite beyond dispute, are yet so clearly certain, that no philosophy which rejects them can hope to stand. Only within the scaffolding of these truths, only on the firm foundation of unyielding despair, can the soul's habitation henceforth be safely built.[13]

[11] E. Tayor, 'The Christian Hope of Immortality'.

[12]

[13] Bertrand Russell, 'Mysticism and Logic'.

'The capacity to adjust and adapt is at its peak in the young, and becomes progressively diminished with advancing age. Natural death can therefore be regarded as the removal from the population of such that are incapable of adjusting to changing evolution.'[14]

This is a very pessimistic view of mans' situation, a view which seems to be wholly dependent upon the 'truths' that Russell mentions. But these 'truths' themselves are mere speculation. Phrases such as 'the vast death of the solar system' and 'universe in ruins' are incompatible with the Christian belief that God is in control of man's past, present and future, that history moves towards a goal, and that the individual person is unique and precious in the sight of God. Russell states a view, which is as pessimistic as that of Martin Heidegger, who states that man is 'Dansein', 'being-in-time', and as such 'Dansein' is also 'being-toward-death'. Thus man's essential state is one of anxiety. Man can only be truly man when he accepts his mortality. On this view, the only reason for man to strive for 'better things' is for the sociological, intellectual, or economic advancement of future generations.

But would man strive at all if his essential state is that of anxiety, and why should mankind hold any ethical values if he accepts as absolute, his mortality. According to Heidegger, man is the only being which truly exists; all other things and animals just 'are' but man truly exists on a much higher category than all other beings. It seems surprising that even a humanist like Heidegger cannot conclude that as man is much 'higher' in this life, than all other creatures, just so man must have a higher destiny than a six-foot hole in the ground and a box smaller than the smallest closet. Another point to note is thatHeidegger's definition of death as the

---

[14] Crew 'The Humanist Outlook'.

end of 'Dansein' as being in-the-world does not demand a logical decision that after death another 'being in eternity is not possible'.

Jean Paul Sartre does not agree with Heidegger's idea that acceptance of one's mortality makes possible a meaningful form of 'being-toward-death'. Sartre believes that death deprives life of any kind of meaning. Life is made up of waitings; even waitings are themselves waiting for something.

> These waitings evidently include a reference to a final term which on principle is never given . . . By means of this final term the recovery of our past would be made once and for all would be being no longer a waiting for being. The whole series is suspended from this final term, the recovery of our past would be made would be made once and for all. We would know for always whether a particular youth experience had been fruitful or ill starred, whether a particular crisis of puberty was a caprice or a real pre-formation of my later engagements, the curve of our lives would be fixed forever.[15]

Unlike Heidegger's optimistic view of acceptance of the inevitability of our death, Sartre believes that this only robs life of all meaning by making it a mere matter of chance whether or not a pattern will emerge in one's life. So he concludes, 'Death is never that which gives life meaning, it is, on the contrary, that which on principle removes all meaning from life.'[16]

I agree with Sartre, death does not give life meaning but life gives death meaning. This life is more than a time of waiting; it is a time for preparing for another better life. With maturity we do

---

15 H.P. Owen, 'The Humanist Outlook'.

16

see a pattern emerging in our lives. Most normal people will admit this, but as Christians we believe there is only One who can see the complete pattern, and that is the One who assures us that this life can give meaning to death.

The main objection I find to Sartre is that the emphasis he puts upon waiting for waiting rules out all hope of contentment within the present moment, thus the majority of human beings would live in a restless state if the waiting theory is true. But the reverse is true. The majority of people find contentment and purpose in their lives, not continuously, but for the greatest percentage of their time here on earth. It must be pointed out, in reply to Heidegger and Sartre, that most normal people do not dwell upon the question of whether or not they are going to accept death in either Heidegger or Sartre's view. Most people are concerned with life and how they will accept it and live it.

References for Chapter 3:

A. E. Taylor, 'The Christian Hope of Immortality'

1. Crew 'The Humanist Outlook'
2. Bertrand Russell 'Mysticism and Logic'
3. H. P. Owen 'The Humanist Outlook'

CHAPTER 4

Christian Attitudes to Death

In the Primitive Church, there was great joy and great hope. St Paul had written that as we are baptised into death with Jesus Christ, then we should surely rise with Christ. For these early Christians, the Gospel message proclaiming the love of God, which had conquered death in the person of Jesus Christ His Son, was a true reality. There were no doubts about those of their numbers who had died, they had gone to be with God (Romans 6:23): 'The wages of sin is death, but the free Gift of God is eternal life in Christ Jesus our Lord.'

But when we come to Augustine in the fifth century, we find that our mortality is a punishment; themes of guilt, remorse, and punishment for our sins are woven into the Doctrines of Creation, Fall, and Incarnation. We can only hope to escape the fires of hell because of the gracious mercy of God the Judge. Yet we do realise that Augustine wrote the most beautiful works about the love of God in Christ Jesus. One need only read his 'Confessions' to realise that he was very aware of God's Grace towards mankind. But for the purpose if this book, we must note his attitude to death.

Augustine stated that, 'The first men were so created, that if they had not sinned, they would not have experienced any kind of death; but having become sinners, they were so punished with death and whatsoever spring from their stock should also be punished by the same death.'[17]

Anselm in the eleventh century also believed that man was created in such a way that there was no necessity for him to die if he had never sinned. God had created man for everlasting happiness, therefore it would be a contradiction to say that God in His wisdom and justice should will that man suffer death for no reason. St Thomas Aquinas and Calvin affirmed the same view. In this view, death is not part of human nature but is 'born' from the evil of human nature. The anguish, pain, and sorrow that accompany death are all part of the punishment for man's sinfulness.

Throughout the Christian centuries, a much more hopeful attitude to death has been expounded. This life is seen as a pilgrimage and death as a passing from one state of existence into another higher state. Irenaeus, in the second century, provided a vocabulary for this concept when he distinguished between the image (*imago*) and the likeness (similitude) of God in man. In this view, man has evolved into a rational, personal creature in the image of God, but he still has to grow and be moulded by a further creative process towards the perfection of his personality, which is his finite likeness to God. It is within his own environment – that is, his own free choice – that man must strive towards that divine likeness.

This pilgrimage concept of life and death continued among some theologians of the Eastern Christian Church. Nineteenth-century Friedrich Schleiermacher developed this thought more fully. Man was not created in a perfect state from which he fell. He was

---

[17] Augustine 'City of God'.

created an immature creature that stood at the beginning of a long process of growth and development. Man is, therefore, still being created and moulded towards the perfection of his personality.

When this approach to the doctrine of the fall and death is expounded, the difference between what man is intended to be and his actual state is clearly shown. Man's state for which God intended is not lost forever but lies before him; it is that for which he must strive in this life. If we hold this view, then our life on earth ceases to be a life of hopelessness, anguish, and torment as in Augustine thought. This life then becomes a time of preparation, of soul-building, and looking forward in hope. The state of anxiety that Heidegger prescribed for being-toward-death becomes a state of striving, a forward-looking state, to a better life after death. It is a time in which we may choose to 'move towards the Divine or return to the level of the beast'.[18] On this view, life is a divinely given opportunity, given to us as individuals and as a race, in which we can move towards real, true humanity as seen in Jesus Christ. There is no pessimism here, and no anxiety – only hope; death is seen as part of the natural process of life, another stage on man's growth towards his chief end.

[18] Augustine, 'City of God'.

CHAPTER 5

Mind–Brain Dependence

It has been argued that human personality is dependent upon the brain. Thus, when the brain ceases to exist, the personality must also cease to exist. We now know because of scientific progress that our bodily functions are dependent upon the brain. Chemical reactions, like those of acetylcholine, pass on and receive messages through the central nervous system to the brain – and from the brain to various parts of our anatomy. For instance, it is my brain that tells my hand to jerk quickly away from a very hot object. It is my brain that controls my breathing, through chemical reactions, which send messages to my brain when the carbondioxide level in my blood becomes too high. My brain 'tells' me to breathe out in order that I may inhale oxygen. If the left side of my cerebral cortex is damaged, this will result in paralysis of the right side of my body. My eyes, ears, movement, sense of taste, and temperature control are all dependent upon that most complex of 'computers', my brain. The argument against life after death, based on mind–brain dependence, seems, at first, positive. So let us begin our counter-argument by asking if the brain depends upon all parts of the body. The answer is much more negative.[19]

If I lose my right arm and leg, the left cerebral hemisphere of my brain will not cease to function, even though, as mentioned earlier, my right side would not function without my left cerebral cortex. The same is true for my eyes, ears, and other parts of my anatomy; my brain can function perfectly well without them. In other words, my eyes, ears, limbs, use my brain, but when they stop using my brain, that brain continues to exist.

What about my personality or mind? It cannot be denied that if my brain is seriously damaged, my personality can be changed beyond recognition – to the observer. However, a personality is much more than that which can be observed. We cannot 'see' inside another person's mind. It is a well-known psychological and physiological fact that very often a person with brain damage or mental illness does not, in fact, think in the same way as he acts. There is a loss of correlation between thinking and acting, between what is observable and what is in that person's mind. We do not know that a person lying on a bed and crudely described as a 'vegetable' has ceased to be the object of his own observations or the subject of his own experience (by this I mean awareness of being). This is why a nurse working with such a person can be heard talking to him, telling him what she is doing next and even 'discussing' the weather with him. We do not know that the conversation is completely one-sided. A lack of observable response is very different from no response. We do not know what is going on in the mind of that patient. To put it more simply, my brain is not

[19] Augustine 'City of God'.

destroyed when parts of my anatomy are, therefore why should my personality (persona) be destroyed when my brain is?[20]

The embryo is utterly dependent upon its environment for survival but nevertheless survives when it is thrust violently out of that environment. We can easily think of the brain as the 'environment' upon which personality is dependent and which it uses in this life. What is to hinder the survival of a personality when it is thrust out of that 'environment' at death? As with the embryo, the personality may depend upon the brain as a temporary and preparatory measure for another kind of existence, as the embryo cannot imagine any other kind of environment, nor know any other kind of existence just so the personality. Fosdick points out that we cannot tell the embryo what this life is like any more than a person who has passed from this life to the next existence can tell us what it is like; therefore, we cannot conceive the knowledge of that other environment. Fosdick also reminds us that 'The man is not the eye, the man uses the eye'. Why then can the personality not use the brain?

In this section, I have been using the words 'mind' and 'personality' synonymously. However, we are all entitled to ask, 'Just what is the personality?' We speak of our friends as having different personalities; we even form opinions of our own personality – meaning our habits, responses to others, disposition and so forth. The word 'person' or 'personality' is given a much deeper meaning when we distinguish between persons and things or

---

[20] References which strengthen the argument. The Christian Hope of Immortality (p.36), Sir James Frazer. The Humanist Outlook (p.257), H.P. Owen. The Humanist Outlook (p. 257), H.P. Owen. Mysticism and Logic (pp. 47–48). Being and Nothingness (p.559). Being and Nothingness (pp. 539 and 540). City of God (Book 13, Chapter 3). The Existence of God (p. 159). The Assurance of Immortality (pp. 78–79).

persons and animals. When we say a person is not to be used merely as an ends to a means but has inherent value as a person, we use the word ‘person’ to denote much more than the popular use of the word ‘personality’ suggests. Is a ‘person’ and a ‘self’ to be given the same meaning? Or do we use the word ‘person’ to denote something with a much deeper and a much different meaning than ‘self’?

1. Augustine ‘City of God’
2. References which strengthen the argument

The Christian Hope of Immortality (p. 36), Sir James Frazer
The Humanist Outlook (p. 257), H. P. Owen
The Humanist Outlook (p. 257), H. P. Owen
Mysticism and Logic (pp. 47–48)
Being and Nothingness (p. 559)
Being and Nothingness (pp. 539 and 540)
City of God (Book 13, chapter 3)
The Existence of God (p. 159)
The Assurance of Immortality (pp. 78–79)

CHAPTER 6

What Does It Mean to Be a Self and to Be a Person?

This seems to be a good place to ask just what it means to be a member of a species – Homo sapiens. Is it any different, apart from obvious physiological and psychological differences, from being a member of any other of the higher animal species? Christians believe that only man, in all creation, was made for eternal communion with his Creator. Man alone is aware of morality and of the beauty within his environment. Thus far we have been speaking of 'man' meaning 'mankind' – a species; to be a self and to be a person is very different from being a member of a species. I will hope to show, in this section, that being a true self and a person is dependent upon being a member of a society of persons.

When we speak of 'self', we mean that part of us which includes, yet exceeds, the anatomical parts that make us recognisable as human beings. We mean that which makes 'me = me' and 'you= you' is an inward awareness of being the same and yet somehow unique among our peers. To be a self, is to be more than an object among other objects, it is more than being the object of observation for others, effecting their experiences and actions within their environment. Existence in that sense can be described and can be ascribed to an infinite number of 'things'. For instance, my experience, sensual at least, can be affected by the absence or presence of a warm fire on a cold day. My actions can be affected by a falling rock, which will crush me if I do not jump clear. But we do not call these things living and experiencing selves.

An experiencing self is a unique self. I can sympathise with someone who is experiencing pain or sorrow, but I cannot experience their pain or sorrow for them. We are capable of observing ourselves analytically as objects of experience and thought. This exercise is difficult. This exercise is difficult and cannot last very long because very soon we as subjects looking at ourselves as objects cease to be subjects and become objects of observation. However, the point is that I can be totally aware of my 'self' in this analytical way, and different from others in a group of people. For a short while, the object of observation is identified with that which is experiencing the observation.

The experience of self is the experience of a thinking, feeling self. All animals can experience, and some can think to a limited extent; we need only think of Skinner's famous pigeons to realise this. However, the personal self who experiences, feels, and thinks is the self who plans, sometimes far into the future, around these three concepts. Every self has a public or outward self, but in each self there is a private, inward, unobservable 'self', which is unique and which is aware of its uniqueness in varying degrees at different times. The 'self' is also capable of observing 'self' in a synthetic manner – as part of a group of other 'selves'.

CHAPTER 7

What Do We Mean When We Say a Human Self Is a Personal Self?

What are we asserting when we say a human self is a personal self? Do we mean that a man is a person, or has personality? A. E. Taylor asks this question, and he reminds us of the words of Boethius more than 1,400 years ago.[21]'A person is an individual substance of rational nature.' Taylor goes on to explain that a person is unitary, unlike a class of students or a flock of sheep. The class or flock has experience in as much as the individual members have experiences. For instance, the class is cold because the individual students are cold. When the class disperses at the end of the day, the individual does not cease to experience but continues to do so; this also applies to a flock of sheep or a herd of goats. But Boethius also stated that man is 'of rational nature' – not just a 'self' but a reasoning, intelligent 'self' and aware of being so.

The discovery of one's personality has a double significance; it is the source of what Kant calls the practical and what he calls the speculative use of reasoning, upon which the possibility of

[21] John Hick 'Death and Eternal Life'.

both science and morality depend. We become aware of our own personality within a society of persons. If, for instance, we lived a life totally deprived of knowledge of and association with other persons, it is unlikely that we would become aware of ourselves as persons, since we would have no experience of persons and therefore nothing on which to gauge what it means to be personal. But it does not follow that we would be unaware of 'self', since 'self' (animal 'self') would still experience pain, cold, heat and so forth. John Hick wrote,

> Personality is essentially interpersonal and consists in our relationships with other persons. Personality is mutual in its very being. The 'self' as ego is solitary, protective, defensive, bound by finite things and bound to be finite. The self as person transcends self as ego – it is mutual and is realised in society with the response of persons to other persons. The 'self' as, person is open to others, self-giving and loving, for it is valuing of one another that we call love that sustains a community. The 'self' as a person is infinite, not bound by finite things, but transcending, overcoming and looking beyond them.[22]

It is when we become aware of our personality that we expect a certain kind of treatment from other persons, and they of us. Genuine morality only becomes possible when we recognise that a person must always be treated as a person because of the value he is in himself, never a means to an end or a mere animal self. Kant focused the attention of the world on this value judgement when he presented it as a basic moral principle, a form of the categorical imperative, that humanity is always to be treated, whether in one's

---

[22] John Hick, 'Death and Eternal Life'.

own person or in the person of any others – never simply as a means but always at the same time as an end. Celsius stated, 'The root of Christianity is its excessive evaluation of the human soul, and it is absurd idea that God takes an interest in man.'

The right of a person to be treated as a person does not depend upon relationships of family, race, colour, or religion; there are no exceptions to this rule. There is not a race (for instance) where we are discharged of our obligation to treat its members as persons, since the right to be treated as a person belongs to the individual. When this obligation is not discharged to a particular race or creed of people, the result can be disastrous as we have witnessed by the actions of Nazi Germany towards the Jewish people. In this way the understanding of morality is closely bound up with the understanding of what a person is and how he is to be treated. This will be discussed further in the next section.

When man discovers his personality, he feels he has a right to ask questions about the nature of his environment, the reasons why some things happen and other things do not, the difference between good and bad. Man's questioning is intelligent, and he expects reasonable answers. He expects a certain pattern of events; the scientist, for instance, forms his hypothesis around an expected set pattern. Science was born out of a pattern of events, and the intelligent pattern of the actions of persons.

Man as a rational, intelligent person has developed over the course of history – from the primitive thinking person who first discovered fire to the now cultured scientific person who has begun to explore the universe; from that savage brutality of the Middle Ages, when it was no rare sight to see a person being burnt alive, to the more sensitive, less savage age we live in, especially in the Western World where the rights of the individual are fiercely protected. A child grows from a feeling being to a thinking being. His personality develops as he learns to control his actions and his behaviour towards other persons, and discovers a pattern in events around him. This process of growth is never completed in this life. A person may die at a very young age or lose all moral control and insight with illness or old age. There are times – that is, during unconsciousness – when moral principles and rational patterns seem to cease. Complete personality seems to be unobtainable in this life. To be a complete person would need to be completely aware of all the patterns of nature in this life, to be always aware of, and in possession of moral insight, and to understand everything in this world in such a way that nothing would be beyond that understanding. For such a complete personality to be possible, we must postulate another existence after this life.

H. E. Fosdick stresses the value of personality and writes, 'If death ends personality, the universe seems to be throwing away with utter heedlessness its most precious possession. Whatever evaluation of the world may be questioned, no one doubts that personality, with its capacities for thought, for character, for love and for creative work, is the crown of all existence . . . Out of what travail. Age long and full of agony has the moral life of man been attained and preserved.'[23]

To emphasise the unreasonableness of the total annihilation of personality, Fosdick uses the illustration of a person making a violin, using infinite labour, gathering the materials and shaping the instrument, only to smash it to pieces at a mere whim.

1. John Hick 'Death and Eternal Life'
2. H. Fosdick 'The Assurance of Immortality'

[23] H. Fosdick, 'The Assurance of Immortality'.

CHAPTER 8

Alternatives to the Survival of the Personality

Alternatives, to personal existence after death, have been offered by many philosophers. Paul Tillich, for instance, suggests that man's immortality is the eternal presence of his earthly life within the mind of God. The divine mind is selective and only retains what is good, rejecting the bad. Evil is only present in the mind of God as that which must be destroyed. Tillich rejects the notion of the survival of the individual person beyond the grave, resting his argument upon the fact that death does occur in the young, thereby preventing the person from reaching his full potential. Eternal life, for Tillich, is a matter of universal participation. If we accept this view, then there would be no concept of personal existence after death, no continued consciousness or relationship to others. What would continue would not be a personal self at all, but a mere memory absorbed into some other self, the other self being God.

That the moral and spiritual gains of persons (i.e. justice, love etc.) are gathered up and made eternal in God even if the individual ceases to exist, as an alternative to personal immortality, will not hold against rational argument. Neither justice nor love can exist in a solitary being whether he is God or man. Justice and love are qualities that are impossible to obtain except in social relationships. God has never revealed Himself as one who wills to do illogical acts such as making a four-sided triangle. Thus, it is more logical to believe that God Himself cannot be just and loving without being just and loving to someone. All the moral values we know are forms of personal activity that would never exist without a social life, and have no meaning apart from relationships between persons. It is surely not possible to think of God hoarding up all the spiritual gains of human personality on the one hand, and of God obliterating those personalities with death on the other hand. Personalities and spiritual gains are interrelated, so much so that if the former are obliterated, then so also must be the latter. Moral qualities cannot survive without the person whose qualities they are.

Tillich's theory of absorption is pantheistic. It would mean that the whole process of creation is just a waste. Men, like all created beings, do participate in God, but mankind participates freely, responsibly, lovingly with God, working towards God's purposes for His creation. Creation is the creating or 'emergence' of particular beings. There is richness in the diversity of created beings, a richness which would be destroyed if all was absorbed into One Being – even if that One Being is the Creator Himself. Therefore, it would be a contradiction to say that God is Creator of all, that He created persons, that He sustains His creation, and then add that He absorbs all the good in that creation into Himself.

The thought of survival in eternity as a 'memory' would fall as far short of Christian hope as Homer's ghosts do. To argue, as Tillich does, of premature death is to forget that a moral interpretation of the New Testament leads to faith in God's love, which is eternal and which does not cease at death. If we believe that in the moral law God has provided a way in which our personalities can strive towards their chief end, it is unreasonable to assert that premature death will end all hope of attaining that goal.

CHAPTER 9

Complete Earthly Bodily Survival

St Thomas Aquinas believed that in the next life we will be exactly the same as we are in this life, even down to our hair and our nails. John Hick quotes Wolfhart Pannenberg who seems to be saying the same as Saint Thomas, namely that the survival of the person after death is the survival of the complete earthly body. This exercise is difficult. This may seem, at first glance, to be the Christian concept of eternal life since the person survives, and this concept carries great difficulties – that is, what happens to the soldier blown to pieces in war? It is a concept that can bring with it the opposite of hope – dread. This exercise is difficult. According to Hick, Pannenberg does say that after death this earthly life will be seen through a new perspective. He states, 'Yet nothing happens in the resurrection of the dead except that which already constitutes the eternal depths of time now, and which is already present for God's eyes – for His view. Thus, through the bridge of our eternal depths of our lifetime, we are, in the present, already identical with the life to which we will be resurrected in the future.'[24]

---

[24] W. Pannenberg.

But if the life we now lead – as Pannenberg states, 'It will be completely different from the way we are now experiencing it' – even if this is the life we lead eternally, then the very thought of eternal life will bring despair. With this concept, there is no hope for the poverty-stricken, the cripple, or the millions of displaced persons. All these people will have to bear their burdens for eternity. Misery is misery whether eternal or temporal, and even if we experience it differently, unless this difference is the destruction of misery – and this according to Hick – Pannenberg does not state. Nobody look forward in hope to an existence of eternal misery. Surely the eternal loving Father will find a way for us, even when the miseries of this life prevent us from reaching our full potential, in the life hereafter which will be free from all earthly miseries.

If Tillich's concept of survival after death seem to make God a 'miser', hoarding to Himself all the virtues of the race, Aquinas and Pannenberg's concept makes God appear to be vindictive, since it seems to say that it is His Will that His creatures suffer misery for all eternity.

The atheist may well agree that there is a kind of personal survival after death, but would argue that there is no need to postulate belief in God in order to hold the belief in the survival of values such as love and goodness of a person after death. Richard Dawkins goes as far as to say that we are all merely vessels containing genes and that the eternity of the race is to be found in the passing on of these genes to the next generation. When we use the words 'soul' and 'person' synonymously as I am now doing, can we not accept that the soul's essential nature is sufficient to persuade us of its eternity? Why not accept Plato's argument that souls alone are apprehending eternal ideas – that is, goodness, love, and truth? Then souls must be capable of sharing in the eternity of those ideas which they apprehend. While we all agree that love, goodness, and so forth, are ideals that are eternal, as Christians we believe we only know that love is eternal because we first know that God is love. Our love, goodness, and so forth, can never be perfect. Our human nature restricts it. How then can we believe that which is imperfect to be eternal?

Love must be more than human love and must have God as its source. If it is a fact that persons can apprehend these values that impress the atheist, then as Christians we can apprehend this, but only because we know that the source of personhood stands out with human limitation and resides in the nature of God. This is why persons can apprehend goodness and love, and this is why persons can survive death.

Plato shows where Tillich and Aquinas are weak. Socrates describes his life as a pilgrimage. He is going to other gods; he is not speaking of the God of the Christian faith, but at least Socrates knows that these other gods are wise and good; they are not miserly or vindictive.

The God of Christianity is personal. He is a Father; the value of personhood belongs to the Fatherhood of God. If we must attempt to describe what personal existence will be like after death, we would do well to agree with Fosdick, who states, 'The best description of the future life yet is to be found in the New Testament. "What eye hath not seen what ear hath not heard, and what hath not entered into the heart of man".'[25]

---

25 J. Hick.

References

The Christian Hope of Immortality 4. p. 40
Death and Eternal Life, p. 50
The Assurance of Immortality, p. 20
Systematic Theology, Vol. III, pp. 395–400
Quoted in Death and Eternal Life, p. 222
The Assurance of Immortality, p. 58

CHAPTER 10

Morality

Morality is bound up in the concepts of good and bad, right and wrong. When an action is praised because it is morally good, or condemned because it is morally bad, a value judgement is being made. Most people, at least those who believe in the objectivity of morals, will agree that value judgements are bound up in moral decision. Thus, when we state that it is right to save a human life 'for instance', we are making a judgement which is based upon the intrinsic value of that human life as a person. For instance, when we condemn the maltreatment of a child, we are basing our judgements upon the intrinsic value of that child as a person.

In morality, the words 'objective' and 'objectivity' can signify three things. Firstly, the actual possession of moral properties by human beings. Secondly, there is the universality of principles or norms. Thirdly, there is the independent existence of moral entities as constituents of a spiritual order. Platonists and Christians maintain that values exist in an intelligible realm. Plato – they exist impersonally as forms or ideas without any personal grounding. Christians – believethey are elements in the self-existent personality of God. Christianity took over the theory of a natural law in morality, from the Stoics. The Stoic concept of natural law was stated by Cicero thus:

> True Law is right reason in agreement with nature; it is of universal application, unchanging and everlasting, it is not allowable to try to repeal any part of it and it is impossible to try to abolish it entirely. We cannot be freed from its obligations by Senate, and we need not look outwith ourselves for an expounder or interpreter of it. And there will not be different laws at Rome and at Athens, or different laws now and in the future, but one eternal and unchangeable law will be valid for all nations, and at all times, and there will be one Master and Ruler, that is, God over us all, for He is the Author of this law, its promulgator and enforcing Judge. Whoever is disobedient is fleeing from himself. And denying his human nature, and by reason of this very fact he will suffer the worst penalties, even if he escapes what is normally considered punishment.[26]

The natural law thus stated means that there is a divine being or principle indwelling nature and ordering all things for the best. Virtue consists in living in accordance with the law, which is discernible by human reason alone, independently of knowledge of its author. The basic principles of morality are available to all men everywhere and are the same for all men everywhere. Therefore, laws of jurisprudence, for instance, which oppose the Natural Law are not valid laws. The divine principle for Christians is God the

---

[26] Cicero.

Father of Jesus Christ, who, as stated earlier, is bsolute goodness and absolute love.

It may be argued that God cannot be the author of the moral law since atheists have lived perfectly good lives, leading to great achievements in, for instance, the realm of social justice. Since these morally good people have no knowledge of God, how can God be responsible in any way for their right actions? Saint Paul provides a reply to the above argument:

'When the Gentiles who do not possess the law carry out its precepts by the light of nature, then although they have no law, they are their own law, for they display the effect of the law inscribed on their hearts.'[27]

In other words, the moral law is dependent upon God ontologically – as its author – but epistemologically morality is autonomous and may be discerned by what Kant calls 'the right use of practical reason'. It may be argued that the laws are different in Athens and in Rome; social anthropology had proved this. In reply, it could be stated that when Desmond Morris, probably the most widely read social anthropologist of his age, speaks of 'pair bonding' in 'The Naked Ape', he notices that. Monogamy is not the accepted concept in every society; a long-term caring relationship is. He also notices that care of the young is a 'law' that runs through human society from very primitive peoples to highly culture races.

An exponent of evolutionary ethics may argue that morality is something that has evolved as society has evolved, that the moral law is that which was found to be necessary for the survival of the species which is social. Against this point of view, we must point out that although evolution shows us how we are developing, evolution does not show us how to develop. Natural selection may choose

---

[27] Ian T Ramsay, 'Freedom and Immortality'.

the fittest, physically, to adapt to a particular environment, but the physical fit is not always the morally good. Nor is the survival of the fittest, the fittest to fulfil a good purpose or end, but merely to survive in this life; many other species in the animal kingdom have survived according to natural selection, but without comprehension of a moral law.

A moral law comprises principles that make an action right or wrong. Good or right actions attract us insomuch as we not only admire the person who does a heroic act but also say, 'How I wish I was like him!' 'How I ought to be like him!' Although a right action may attract us, we still experience conflict; we feel that we want to do that which is morally good, and at the same time feel drawn towards that which is morally bad. Swinburne points out that this element of free choice in moral actions is compatible with beings of free will, since a being has free will only if his intentional actions are not fully determined;[28] the limitation of free will being that if the choice or right or wrong is up to a person, then he must comprehend, in some way, that which is morally good; even if he is inclined to do that which is morally bad.

Arguing against human behaviour being completely predictable, Ian I. Ramsay states, 'If only we had the wisdom to know all the cause factors, behaviour would be completely predictable.'[29]

I agree with Ramsay. We can never know all the cause factors in a situation; human behaviour is not fully determined. In many ways human behaviour has been shown to be unpredictable. For instance, we may say that from his verbal utterances, behaviour, interests, and so forth, it was predictable that James Smith (policeman) would someday enter the Christian ministry. But we cannot say

---

28 Swinburne, 'The Existence of God'.

29 Swinburne, 'The Existence of God'.

why he chose to go at that particular time. Why not a year ago, or a year from now? Why enter the ministry at all? Could he not still remain a policeman, preach the gospel, and give pastoral care as a lay-preacher? I also agree with Ramsay when he says that human behaviour, although not completely predictable, is not completely free. To say otherwise would be to deny the natural law theory of morals.

Ramsay goes on to say that moralists claim a 'free choice' or a responsible decision 'contains something extra besides the actualising of one alternative rather than the other'. But he never really goes on to say what that 'something extra' really is, apart from saying on the following page that it is something 'more than special temporal events' and 'has something to do with our sense of obligation'[30] I would suggest that this 'something extra' that gives us limited free choice must be, as mentioned above, a pull towards wrong while having the knowledge of what is right – the moral law in other words.

We have noted that moral values (a) attract us and (b) leave us with limited free choice of whether or not we will act upon their attraction. So you might ask what the difference is between postulating Platonic forms as the authors of the moral law, or postulation of the personal God of Christianity as its author. I will dare to argue for the latter!

Platonic forms may attract, but they do not put us under obligation; the element of obligation is not prominent in Plato as it is in, say, Kant; thus it is reasonable to think that the moral conscience requires that we combine the Platonic and Kantian attitude by viewing values, not simply as ideas that attract a natural desire but also as facts that impose an unconditional obligation, what Kant

30

calls 'the categorical imperative'. We are not only attached to values that are good; we feel obliged to exercise these values. As mentioned earlier, if we observe someone who is conspicuously good, in as far as we are attracted to him we may say 'How I wish I was more like that!' And so it can be concluded that moral values are not only ideals that attract but also, indeed, facts that impose unconditional obligation.

The fact that we aspire to moral goodness, however, does not prove the existence of that goodness, since we could just as easily aspire to something that is nothing more than a 'whim'. A 'whim' can be irrational, phobic, or compulsive. For instance, I may suddenly decide for no good reason that I should eat nothing but eggs for a month; I may feel this compulsion quite strongly, but in no way would I feel obligated to eat eggs only for a month. I would feel no obligation either to hold that 'whim' or to carry it into action, whereas goodness places us under obligation and under constraint. If we feel that an action is morally bad, we also feel constrained from committing that action. For instance, I may want to be disloyal to my dearest friend, but the lack of goodness in such an action would constrain me from that act. It could be argued that it would need more than a lack of goodness in such an act to constrain me from committing the disloyal action. I would agree with this but add that just as goodness and love are held together in the nature of God, they are held together in all personal relationships. The love spoken of here is 'agape', described as awareness of the value and response to the value of persons.

We cannot equate this goodness or Absolute goodness to which we feel attracted and which places us under obligation with Platonic forms. In this life, in this world, moral ideals are found in persons and not in things. How can a person ever participate in or hope to reflect a goodness which is impersonal? The personal God of Christianity is that ultimate good that both attracts and places us under obligation. When we think of the obligatory nature of such actions as keeping promises, telling the truth, loving my neighbour, we conclude that these are actions for which no utilitarian justification can be given. Such actions are obligatory, according to Kant, only if they add to the perfection or lead nearer to the perfection of the universe, what Kant calls the 'summum bonum'. The moral strivings of Christians are made in response to the revelation of the will of God in Jesus Christ who, in His Person, embodies the moral law and reveals that God's will for man is goodness and love.

It seems reasonable at this point and with regards to what has been written to sum up just what has been said about moral values. First, the natural law or awareness of good and bad flows from the eternal love of God. It is not necessary to know God in order to be aware of moral values. Ontologically, morality is dependent upon God, but epistemologically morality is autonomous. Secondly, the attractive and obligatory nature of moral values is well suited to our creaturely existence since, as Swinburne states, 'it is reasonable that God made persons with bodies, since if an agent has a body that is the part of the world through which his intentions are executed and through which he acquires knowledge'.[31] The knowledge referred to here is the knowledge of the laws of nature, expected states of the world, and the effects he/she produces with his/her actions in the world. Swinburne also states, 'We cannot regard moral goodness as 'our good' unless we already feel its claims and chose it for its own distinctive excellence.'

[31] Swinburne, 'The Existence of God'.

Thirdly, limited free will and obligation are very important, if not crucial, to any natural law theory; since if we were perfectly good, we would not feel the 'pull' towards good since we would have no inclinations towards bad. But since we are aware of both, then we have limited free choice, and the obligation that morally good actions place upon us is the 'pull' towards good.

If we remember that man's chief end is to glorify God, or to reflect the divine nature, and the command 'Be ye perfect even as your Father in Heaven is perfect', it is not difficult to realise how impossible it is for us, as finite creatures, to achieve our real 'goal' in this life. The very imperfections of our nature contradict the fact that perfection is our 'goal'. It may be easy, at times, to carry out this so-called second-order values, but the claims on our inner will (i.e. no envy, no anger etc.) show how far we all fall short of that perfection. But we have been given means of growing towards our 'goal' by the knowledge of the moral law as being not only the command but the very nature of God.

Philosophers over the centuries have put forward the moral argument for immortality. It would be impossible to look at all these arguments in this book; we will take a little time to look at three of the best known works on this subject.

CHAPTER 11

The Moral Argument for Life after Death

Plato

The moral argument goes further than any others in requiring a God of love and life after death – a God of love who will remedy our weakness and grant us the happiness of life with Him forever. Plato argued for the immortality of the soul being somehow bound up with the concepts of good and bad, with human actions, reasoning, and so forth, in this life.

Plato's theory of the soul formed part of a characteristic theory of reality, which was the outcome of more than a century of speculation on Being and Becoming. In his doctrine of ideas or forms, Plato reached the concept of a mode of being that was eternal; not in the sense of Parmenides – that of persisting changelessness neither through time; nor in the sense of Heraclitus who said that all is in 'flux' like a river continually changing. Plato's concept was one of absolute timelessness; truths and ideas are eternal; they are unlike things that exist in space and perish through time; they are eternal in a sense that they have no relation to time at all. The objects of sense perception are involved in flux and are only objects in as much as they exemplify some universal nature. Plato writes, 'And these you can touch and see and perceive with the senses, but the unchanging things you can only perceive with the mind – they are invisible and are not seen.'[32]

Therefore, it is reason that discloses to us a world of true reality, which is out with time and space. The status of the soul in Platonic thought is somewhere between the eternal world of intelligible reality; ideas or forms being the only true reality (Being) and the quasi – real world of Becoming, for instance – what we have to do with in sense perception and everyday living. This exercise is difficult. The soul is related to these two worlds. As Becoming, it is related to the concrete observable things in this world; its true kinship is with the eternal ideas or forms. It is this true kinship that inspires the soul in its quest towards absolute beauty, love, virtue, and the likes. But the soul itself is not an idea or form; souls are immortal but not eternal in the sense of ideas. It is by partaking of these ideas that the soul appropriates their content and makes the beautiful the virtuous, the element in which the soul lives; thus the soul becomes a partaker of the eternal nature of these ideas, and Plato quotes his master's words as follows:

> But there is a further function Gentlemen, said Socrates, which deserves your attention. If the soul is immortal it demands our care not only for that part of time we call life, but of eternity. And the danger from this point of view does indeed appear to be awful. If death had only been the end of all, the wicked would have a good bargain in dying for they would have been happily quit, not only of their body, but of their own evil together with

[32] Cicero quoted in Summa Theologica.

> their souls. But now in as much as the soul is manifestly immortal, there is no realise or salvation from evil except the attainment of the highest virtue and wisdom. For the soul, when on her progress to the world below takes nothing with her but nature and education; and these are said greatly to benefit or greatly to injure the departed at the very beginning of his journey thither.[33]

But in reading the Phaeton, we are made aware that Plato points beyond his master Socrates to the truths he taught whereas the Christian points directly at his Master who embodies these truths in His Person. Platonic dualism between body and soul is very different from the Christian concept of the body as the temple of the spirit, and precious in the eyes of Christ who Himself became man. The radical distinction which Plato makes between Being and Becoming would make an Incarnation of these truths and values, which he points to, impossible. However, Plato and Aristotle held the view that immortality was influenced by and depended upon how we use our reason towards striving for the good, the beautiful, and so forth, in this life.

Both Plato and Aristotle held that the realisation of man's immortality was open only to philosophers, and this exercise is difficult. The term 'philosopher' had a wider meaning, when used by these ancient Thinkers, than it has in English today, it still excluded the majority of people. It is to be noted that from the earliest days of Christianity the belief in a future life was a belief of the ordinary people and not the intellectual only. The link between our final destinies in Christian thought is established by the intervention of God who rewards the righteous and punishes

[33] De republica, 1112.

the wrong doers like a judge. The important point here is that the judgement is from first to last by God alone, not by any impersonal Platonic forms or 'nature of things'. It is a judgement which will be good because it is made by the highest form of Wisdom, the Creator of all things who has revealed Himself to be goodness, love, and holiness in His Son Jesus Christ.

1 Cicero quoted in Summa Theologica
2 Ian T. Ramsay, 'Freedom and Immortality'
3 De republica, 1112

CHAPTER 12

St Thomas Aquinas

Like Plato and Aristotle, St Thomas Aquinas developed a teleological theory of ethics; the idea of being good being paramount. For all three writers, human acts derive their moral quality from their relationship to men's final end. But as Copleston reminds us, 'The God of St. Thomas' natural theology is first cause and the Creator, as well as final cause'.[34]

For Saint Thomas it is not Platonic forms but the God of Christianity who is the first and final cause of all there is. From consideration of Saint Thomas' Doctrine of Teleology, that all agents work from an end which is good, we must consider how mankind fits into the picture. How does man act for his good end in a way peculiar to man? According to Aquinas, that which distinguished man from other earthly creature is man's possession of reason, and a free will which is a function of reason and will. He distinguishes between 'acts of man' and 'human acts'. Acts of man are non-rational acts that would include reflex actions. Human acts are those things that we do after the application of some degree of thought.

---

[34] Copleston, 'A History of Philosophy'.

So it can be seen that human reason is an important factor (S.T.1–11, 91a 1).

All agents work for an end, which is good. It is good because it is the perfection of the agent according to its nature, and also it is the object of the right appetite of the agent. When we consider the rational nature of man, we see that the end and good for which man acts must be understood by man to be good, and this good is the object of his will; thus man acts for that end which he perceives to be good. The statement that all men work for good must be understood as meaning that all men act for that which they understand rightly or wrongly, to be good. Thus actions of men for the good induce actions that are properly good and understood as such; actions which are understood; actions which are understood as good but which are in truth not good and actions which are both bad and are understood to be so. Thus the desires that are satisfied by the actions of man may be ordinate or inordinate.

For Aquinas the whole world exists for the glory of God; this includes human beings with their potential for action. Thus human conduct is subordinate to an end out with itself. God acts and obligation exists only through their relation to their intrinsic end. But the perfection of all creatures is for the glorification of God, and the whole moral life is founded on the will's movement towards the good. But what is the concrete good of man? Copleston explains Saint Thomas' concept of man's good as follows:

> The statement that the will always chooses sub species boni, that it chooses a goal, real or apparent, draws attention to the fundamental drive of all our conscious choices; the drive or impulse to self-development or self-perfection to happiness. As this natural impulse does not depend on or necessarily carry with it an implicit

> conception of man's objective good in the concrete, it is possible to form a mistaken idea of it.[35]

Copleston has used the word 'happiness' to denote man's good, and this is a term that Saint Thomas uses in as much as 'beatitude' may be translated as 'happiness'. For Aquinas, human happiness does not consist of carnal pleasures, in honours, glory, wealth, in worldly power, in goods of the body, and is not seated in the senses.[36]Thomas denied that the final good of man consists in any or all these apparent goods precisely because on their own or even when taken together they are held not to properly fulfil and perfect the rational. Each of these apparent goods may satisfy some inordinate desire in man, but ultimately they must fail to satisfy man's proper desire for happiness. This is because each of these goods is a good, which is followed for the sake of something else; they do not serve to culture or perfect reason, which is held to be the most significant aspect of man's nature; thus none of these can be the perfecting of man according to his nature.

Ultimate human happiness does not consist in acts of moral virtue; this exercise is difficult. One may expect that such acts would constitute the good of man. But these acts are always done for some other better effect than themselves – namely, the glory of God. Thus the good, which is man's final end, is not created by the acts of men but is a good in a much more extrinsic sense as something which man must strive to attain. God, as the final common good, precedes in both causing and being, and so it is a good which is not created by the acts of any agent but must be achieved and obtained by the acts of an agent . . . As Aquinas states, 'None can reach

35 Copleston, 'A History of Philosophy'.

36 Summa contra Gentiles, 111, Chapter 3.

happiness without good will and the loves of one who sees God inevitably fall in with the Divine Plan.'[37]

For Aquinas it is the possession of God that actualises man's potentialities in the highest possible degree and in the most complete manner. But as he was convinced that this possession is impossible without supernatural grace, that it transcends the natural powers of man and that without revelation we cannot know that it is attainable and constitutes the actual final end of man, the conclusion inevitable suggests that the moral philosopher, in a narrow sense, cannot be sure what man's supreme good or final end really is. And this conclusion would create difficulties in a theological ethic in which the concept of a final end plays such a large part. Human acts are declared to be morally good or bad in so far as they are/ are not compatible with the attainment of this end. Aquinas did not think that without revelation it is possible to have any knowledge of the good for man. According to Saint Thomas, 'The last and perfect happiness of man cannot be otherwise than the Divine Essence'.[38]However, even if one knows nothing of the Beatific Vision, one is perfectly capable of seeing that some acts conduce to man's perfection, to the development and perfection of his nature, and that others are incompatible with this.

For Aquinas, happiness as a perfect and sufficient good could not be attained in this life because we could not exclude all the evil and privation in this life, such as ignorance on the part of the uneducated poor, inordinate affliction on the part of the appetite, and afflictions of the body. Also, the perfect good, as desired by man, must be a permanent thing; but the goods of this life are transient as this life is transient (S.T. 1–II 9 5 a 3). The natural end

---

37 Summa contra Gentiles, 111, Chapter 3.

38 S.T.I. 1 – 11 q 31 s 8.

for man is perfectly human; however, in that it is an end to which man is properly inclined and which man can strive towards by full use of his natural processes.

Aquinas thought of man as tending naturally towards his perfection, towards the actualisation of his potentialities as man, towards his final end or goal. He thought of practical reason as discerning the acts necessary to this end, as ordering them and forbidding their contraries. In this sense obligation is imposed by the practical; reason, binding the free will to perform the acts necessary for the attainment of the final good for man and to abstain from acts which are incompatible with its attainment.

Kant, on the other hand, divides principles of conduct into two classes: the hypothetical and the categorical imperatives. The hypothetical imperative is a principle of conduct that is accepted but not on its own merits but as a rule for gaining some serious end. The categorical imperative is a principle that is accepted on its own merits and therefore is done for a principle. The formal criterion for a principle being accepted on its own merits is this. Anyone who accepts it as his principle of conduct can consistently desire that everyone else can also make it their principle and act upon it. This supreme principle is what Kant calls the categorical imperative or moral law.

For Aquinas, the practical reason and speculative reason are not different powers as in Kant. Speculative reason is concerned with the knowledge and consideration of truth, while practical reason is concerned with the application of what is apprehends either in moral conduct, artistic or technical skills (S.T.Ia.7q.11.). The moral imperative is not therefore a problematic hypothetical imperative, as in Kantian thought. It does not say ‘if you want to attain this or that end you must take these means’. For Saint Thomas the moral imperative says, 'You necessarily seek this end because you know you are a human being, therefore you ought to do this and ought to do that.' In this sense, the imperative is unconditional and absolute. Kant would call it an asserter hypothetical imperative, and he considered that this imperative was not equivalent to the categorical imperative recognised by the moral consciousness. But Aquinas was convinced that though the moral imperative is in a real sense unconditional and absolute, a rational analyses and account of obligation can be given which shows the part it plays in human life. According to Saint Thomas, all seek happiness in an intermediate sense, and the moral imperative directs the taking or accepting of the means to this end. Among the means is the discovery of what happiness signifies, and for Aquinas, happiness is in the possession of God.

The arguments of Saint Thomas have at least the advantage in beginning from the concrete empirical facts, which are open to observation rather than from abstract ideas. Natural theology played an important part in theological philosophy by linking the theologian's world with the world of experience; or in other words, it showed the connection between theological discourse and everyday discourse, providing a 'foundation' for theological discourse that should not be severely frowned upon. Moreover, if Aquinas method could be shown that there is a God, that He is beneficent, and that man has an immortal destiny, then it would follow that in all probability God would reveal Himself more fully, and so revealed theology gets a flying start. Whereas if we wipe out natural theology, revealed theology, philosophically speaking, is left as an odd phenomena, and the probability that it is mere illusion becomes vastly increased, especially among anti-theists.

However, few philosophers and theologians now accept the belief that the existence of God and life after death can be rationally demonstrated. The attempt to move from empirical evidence to 'transempirical' conclusion involves a logical jump that has never been satisfactorily explained. A convincing theological objection to natural theology, with which I agree, is that natural theology takes its stand on the finitude of our finite existence. Contemporary philosophers and theologians, on the whole, reckon more seriously than their predecessors, with the finitude of human existence.

In my opinion, natural theology is incompatible with the finitude of our race. To be finite is to live with risk and uncertainty. This is clear from our everyday experience of life in which we have to commit ourselves to policies of action without all the complete knowledge of all the relevant circumstances, and still less of all the consequences which are caused by our action. We see life only from our limited standpoint, so it follows that we cannot know the whole ultimate truth about it. Therefore, to claim or demand a guaranteed certitude, based on the rational nature of man that there is life after death is to refuse to acknowledge our own finitude, for as Saint Paul reminds us in 1 Corinthians 13: 12f, we do not see 'face-to-face' but 'in a mirror dimlyly'.

The main objection I have to Saint Thomas' argument is that it begins from the side of mankind. In our knowledge of God, it is He who takes the initiative, not man. He makes Himself known to us and so the movement comes from His side and not from us to Him. Saint Thomas, in opposition to this, starts from the point of man and man's desire for the fulfilment of his potentiality as man and seeks to find a way to God and to life after death. Another theological objection to the natural theology questions if it is proper to be talking about God in terms that are available in a deductive argument. This is the counterpart of the philosophical objection that questions the move from the empirical to the 'transempirical' (a word coined by some theologian or philosopher).

We can, however, take objections to Saint Thomas too far and result in making man a purely passive recipient of the knowledge of God thereby leaving no room for reciprocity or appropriation. Such objections are exaggerated when they rob man of his God-given gifts of rationality, responsibility, and personal being . . . Even so it still seems clear that our knowledge of God and life after death can never be like our knowledge of the facts of this world. Our knowledge of the facts of this world is gained by our active discovery of them. Since God Himself is the upreme active principle, He does not wait for our active discovery of Him but presents and manifests Himself in an active manner within the history of mankind. We can only speak analogically about God from our experiences of this world.

Therefore, I conclude that Saint Thomas does not demonstrate the reality of God and life after death but creates a 'bridge' between everyday knowledge and experience of the world – and that knowledge is the content of faith. Plato, Aristotle, and Aquinas argued that morality demands eternal life as man's final goal or end. The pursuit of happiness no less than the response to value claims requires the presumption of God and of life after death.

CHAPTER 13

Kant

Emmanuel Kant argued that in this life goodness is not always accompanied with happiness. But it ought to be. Therefore, we must postulate another life in which this defect will be remedied. But we must also postulate God, since only He possesses both goodness and a power to apportion the rewards of virtue and to create the environment in which uninterrupted happiness will be possible.

I do agree with Kant that happiness is not always the 'reward' for goodness. Very often moral goodness involves the sacrifice of a life, a sacrifice for which no reward is obvious either in the saving of another life or in happiness for the person involved in the morally good action. We need only think of the tsunamis a few years ago in Japan where both the rescuers and those in need of rescue drowned. However, this does not 'take away' from the goodness or the virtue of the volunteer rescuers. Very often moral goodness is found in the most poverty-stricken, underprivileged homes and localities where happiness seems very much lacking in the lives of the people involved. Kant says,

> Inasmuch as virtue and happiness together constitute the possession of the highest good for a person, and happiness in exact proportion to morality (as the worth of a person and his worthiness to be happy) constitutes that of a possible world, the highest good means the whole, the perfect good wherein value is always the supreme good being the condition having no condition superior to it. Though happiness, though something pleasant to him who possesses it, is not of itself absolutely good in every respect but always presupposes conduct in accordance with the moral law as its condition.[39]

Kant's words 'happiness in exact proportion to morality' gives rise for query. This happiness cannot be that which we would like to have. Not one of us would like to have happiness proportioned according to our devotion to duty, since none of us are completely devoted to duty; none of us are perfectly good and virtuous. Christian theism affirms that man's final end is a participation in the goodness or holiness of God, so our moral strivings in this world are always inadequate. Even if I succeed in fulfilling the eternal demands of the moral law viz. the Ten Commandments, one could never hope to fulfil the inner demands of the Sermon on the Mount. Thus, Kant's concept of happiness as being the complete condition that one has or feels when in complete accord with the moral law is much less adequate than Saint Thomas' concept of happiness as far as Christian theism is concerned.

Kant also argued from happiness to immortality, but he did not realise that this argument required the postulation of an infinitely personal God. Having said that the aim of the moral life is perfect obedience to the moral law, he states,

---

[39] Kant, 'Critique of Practical Reason'.

> But complete fitness of the will to the moral law is holiness, which is a perfection of which no rational being is at any time capable. But since it is required as practically necessary, it can be found in an endless progress to that complete fitness; on principles of pure practical reason, it is necessary to assume such a practical progress as the real object of our will. This infinite progress is possible however, only under the presupposition of an infinitely enduring existence and personality of some rational being: this is called the immortality of the soul.[40]

On the one hand, Kant postulates immortality for the achieving of perfection yet. On the other hand, he implies that perfection will always evade our grasp; this I find to be contradictory. Yet a contradiction on the plain of morality is inevitable. In this life, we do not know good apart from knowing evil, because even the most saintly person faces the struggles of temptation. I agree with H. P. Owen, who states, 'If the thread of sin did not exist, our characters would stagnate.'[41]The holiness that we strive to reflect is God's holiness. We can never be holy in ourselves, and this exercise is difficult. The Christian received his morality from the will of God; he is not continually aware of striving to reflect the holiness of God. God acts through us in Word and Spirit within our sphere of understanding, by giving us the power to discern and the freedom to choose between right and wrong. This is why we are able within our finite existences to strive to live in accordance with God's holy will. God's holiness is love He created and redeemed us out of that love that we might share in the love, which is His nature. Therefore,

---

[40] I. Kant, 'Critique of Practical Reason'.

[41] H.P. Owen, 'The Moral Argument for Christian Theism'.

it is God's will; God's love is the imperative of the moral law. Owen states, 'Morality is fulfilled in the belief that the whole life of duty is a debt of gratitude to God for His great love in creating us to share in His Perfection.'[42]

A point to note here is that the whole of Kant's moral system rests on two theses. Firstly, nothing is unconditionally good except the good will. Secondly, the good will is something that subjects itself to duty for duties' sake. Therefore, one would expect Kant to be horrified at the idea of the reward in the external condition of happiness. His ethical principles point to the fact that virtue has its own reward and that any idea of reward in morality is wrong.

As Owen points out, we cannot argue categorically from happiness to God and immortality, but even a hypothetical argument can show that the rejection of the hypotheses renders the moral life contradictory. But if we start from the major premise that God exists, then we can become categorical. We can only argue from happiness to God and life after death if happiness is interpreted in oral terms and allows us to posit communion with God as our ultimate good. We must start from a concept of happiness much more profound than the Kantian concept, integrating the truths of Kantian deontology with the teleological ethics of Plato, Aristotle, and Aquinas.

The Christian regards happiness as the surrender of the total self to God's joy-giving love. Christian happiness often comes in the form of 'that peace which passes all understanding', which comes from communion with God. Thus, to argue from happiness, we must postulate God as our beatitude since mere human 'perception' could not satisfy our desires. If we start from a non-religious premise and take morality as man's chief end, then it is

---

42 H.P. Owen, 'The Moral Argument for Christian Theism'.

not difficult to see that this is end is unachievable. We are limited finite beings, imperfect by nature, yet perfection is our final goal; it is an obligation, a command 'Be ye perfect even as your Father in heaven is perfect'. Moral failure is universal; even Kant recognised this. Therefore, there must be another existence out with the present temporal limitations that restrict us in this life – an existence in which these limitations are no more effective and we are capable of fulfilling the command of Christ.

The humanist could agree that society is evolving towards man's perfection. But there is no real point in arguing that greater knowledge, scientific or otherwise, leads to greater virtue when the knowledge of our present age does not support this; in fact, very often the reverse is true. We can never hope for perfection if it is founded upon human nature alone. Only a divine nature that is absolute goodness and ultimate love can make this perfection possible.

Arguments from happiness to immortality are exposed to the question about the fulfilment of absolute values. We may desire such a fulfilment. But how do we know that such fulfilment will occur in finite creatures? The Kantian argument – while proving that if God exists, He will reward our obedience to His will – does not prove that God exists. When we equate happiness with virtue, are the theist's conclusion secure? Do we have to admit that if God exists He must be our beatitude but that moral teleology cannot prove His existence? It is with these questions in mind that Kroner criticises Kant:

> However the categorical imperative commands us to act in such a manner that we will the maxim of our action to become a general law. It does not demand the

> achievement of holiness or the complete adequacy of the will to the moral law. It may be possible for us to do our duty and yet impossible for us to achieve holiness. Only if we are over and above the categorical imperative subject to a command to become holy does, according to Kant's argument, the notions of immortality have practical objectivity. The reason why Kant's argument for immortality carries little conviction is not a logical flaw, but I think that we do not recognise the command to achieve holiness as a law that we can possibly choose to satisfy.[43]

If we think of God's holiness, which is love, then we realise that the divine indicative (I love you) precedes the divine imperative (Be ye holy). In Jesus Christ we have the fulfilment of the love of God towards man (indicative) and the fulfilment of the divine imperative (command.) Therefore, we are 'over and above the categorical imperative subject to the command to become holy'. But when we, to the best of our finite ability, respond wholeheartedly to that command, it ceases to be a command and becomes, instead, a life of gratitude towards a loving Father who is, in His nature, goodness, love, holiness, righteousness, and has revealed Himself to be so in the Incarnate Lord. Therefore, God is our beatitude, and moral teleology cannot prove His existence. He comes Himself in Word and Spirit and makes Himself known to us.

---

[43] Kroner, 'Kant'.

CHAPTER 14

Virtue

It has been argued that virtue, on ethical grounds, must be disinterested. Virtue that is for gain is not virtue. Christianity has been criticised for teaching as a means of avoiding hell and gaining heaven; it has been said that because of this teaching Christian virtue is not true virtue. So Kant complained that the introduction of 'religious sanction' entirely destroys the sublimity of the moral law. In reply to these criticisms, it must be pointed out that disinterested doing of good just because it is good will not help man to withstand the most severe temptations of this life unless it is joined to a categorical command (the divine imperative) and inescapable obligation (the divine indicative). For the Christian, as mentioned throughout this paper, the command is 'Be ye perfect . . .' The inescapable obligation is in the form of gratitude to God for all He is and all that He has done for us.

What would happen if we did completely divorce morality from 'religious sanction'? Would we not destroy the very meaning of virtue? As mentioned earlier, Aquinas pointed out that man chooses what he thinks to be good at a particular time, but man's 'good' is not always truly good. Virtue must be obligatory and involve the recognition of the One who is absolute goodness and to whom we are answerable for our decisions. If this was not so, then we would be left with nothing but opinions of men as to what constitutes the good and the right, and of course, these opinions of good and right can be changed to suite a particular purpose or the aims of a particular society. We have already seen how men can justify their own idea of 'the good' in Nazi Germany where thousands of Jews were exterminated for the 'good' of society, for the creation of a super Aryan race. Then there are more recent events in Poland, Africa, and other places where the freedom of people was and in some places still is being curbed, and where people go hungry for the 'good' of the state. These are only two examples of how man can justify his own ideas of good, but hundreds of more examples can be found in the history of mankind.

The Christian law of virtue is laid down and regulated by Christ's two great commands in the New Testament. We are commanded to 'love God with all your heart and all your soul and your neighbour as yourselves'. We are not to love God for the sake of any benefits we may gain but simply because He is God. Obedience to these commands does not make virtue into some kind of currency that we can 'cash in' to gain life after death. We need only to consider the nature of the reward to discover this. The reward for loving God and loving neighbour in this life is eternal life, an eternity of loving relationships, which is much deeper and truer than in this life. This reward would not appeal to one who was completely self-centred because if he does not love God and neighbour selflessly in this life without seeking reward, then it is no reward at all to be given an even greater capacity to love in the life hereafter.

Christianity does not deny the proposition that virtue has its own reward but believes that the 'reward' for virtue in this life is another existence where all the drawbacks to virtuous living will be no more. Therefore, we conclude that without a grasp of divine grace and the divine imperative within the moral order, happiness quickly becomes self-centred. Without references to well-being, duty becomes oppressive.

This life is a time of preparation, of soul-building for the time when the Christian will be able to reflect the goodness of God in the life after death. On this view, morality demands eternal life as man's final end. But how does the morally good atheist fit into all this? Christians and atheists both journey through this life, each apparently making the same journey. But for the atheist, this life is all there is. Any choice he makes between good and bad will be determined by what he thinks is good for humanity in this life only. He would argue that the moral conscious of man has been cultivated by the evolution and needs of society. He would state that he does look beyond this life in a way because the good or bad actions that he performs will influence the lives of future generations when he is dead. But for the atheist the journey along the road of this life leads nowhere. The Christian also believes that his actions will influence future generations, but for him the 'pull' towards good and the realisation of what is bad or wrong are God-given gifts to help him on his soul-building journey towards the 'Celestial City'.

These two, Christians and atheists, do not have different experiences along the road. Both experience emotional joys and sorrows. Both have the same expectations about what life will entail, but the goal is different; the trains of life are viewed differently. The Christian realisation of good and bad, right and wrong, is realised by Christian revelation.

CHAPTER 15

Christian Revelation

At the beginning of this section, it was stated that the moral argument goes further than any others in requiring a God of love and life after death. However, such an argument can only reveal God and His purpose for man in a limited sense. The only true revelation is given by God Himself in the person of Jesus Christ – Immanuel. In that Historic Person we see humanity, true humanity, as God intends us to be; but in that same Person we see God Incarnate (Immanuel).

We read in the Gospel according to Saint John (1: 18), 'No one has ever seen God; the only Son, who is in the bosom of the Father, He has made Him known.'

Jesus reveals God to us, and reveals Him to be holy, loving, just, and good. H. P. Owen writes, 'Christian Revelation deepens the insight that nature itself affords.'

In Jesus the nature of God is revealed; thus the nature of morality is revealed. Also revealed is the way in which the experience of forgiveness resolves our feelings of guilt over our transgressions of the moral law. This is possible only through faith in the Incarnation and Atonement – Atonement that was worked out on the cross at Calvary. In His life of obedient self-sacrifice, Jesus embodies the goodness and love of God. We are challenged to be like Him; we are attracted to the value claims embodied in His person, and we are placed under obligation by that challenge, which is the self-giving love of God.

Jesus' command to love one's enemies is a mere 'balm' for peacemaking within society. It has a religious motive (Matt. 5: 44–45). We are commanded to love our enemies because such love is shown by God Himself who freely bestows His gifts on the just and the unjust. This dependence of ethics upon religion is evident in the teaching of Saint Paul (Rom. 12, well-known words).

If we interpret the New Testament in moral terms, we find that it leads us to a love that is eternal and does not cease at death. Christian love is agape and flows from the love of God. It is deepened and strengthened by the revelation of God in Christ who exemplified that love in its fullest degree. Love is the bond – the hypostatic union – within the eternal fellowship of the Father, Son, and Holy Spirit. The Christian is united to his Master through the Holy Spirit, in that bond of love, the love that was revealed in the history of mankind, in the person of Jesus Christ. H. P. Owen states, 'Each item in this sequence is a link in a chain that binds man to God, earth to Heaven, time to Eternity, life and immortality.'[44]

If, as Christians, we accept who Christ is and the values which He embodies, then it would be illogical not to accept His promise of eternal life: 'In my father's house there are many mansions . . . I go to prepare a place for you . . .' The resurrection of Christ brings with it the resurrection of all believers. We will live a life of eternal fellowship with Him, a life in which we shall reflect the divine

[44] H.P. Owen

perfection, but only reflect it, because for all eternity God is Lord of all and we are His creatures.

In Christian belief in life after death, there is no thought of the believer ever becoming divine, only a sure and certain hope of resurrection from the dead. Life after death is a gift from God, just as the love that we are commanded to give is also a gift from God, and not something we possess on our own.

Revelation fulfils the concept of beatitude. Reason can suggest that our highest good or goal is to achieve perfection in an everlasting life with God, but reason can never convince us that – that goal exists.

Section 2

1. H. P. Owen

References

De republica III 2
Romans 2: 14–15
The Existence of God, chapter 9
Freedom and Immortality, p. 14
Freedom and Immortality, p. 19
Freedom and Immortality, p. 29
The Existence of God, p. 160
The Existence of God, p. 198
Dialogues of Plato, p. 227 (79)
Dialogues of Plato, p. 255
A History of Philosophy, vol. II, part 2, p. 148

Copleston – Aquinas, p. 192

Critique of Practical Reason, pp. 214–215

Critique of Practical Reason, p. 215

Critique of Practical Reason, pp. 225–226

The Moral Argument for Christian Theism, p. 101

The Moral Argument for Christian Theism, p. 66

Kant (Kroner), p. 166

The Moral Argument for Christian Theism, p. 119

The Moral Argument for Christian Theism, p. 113

CHAPTER 16

The Problem of Evil

The problem of evil would seem to be a very strong argument against the previous section of this book. Therefore, it is logical to discuss the problem now. The argument against the existence of God and in life after death because of the problem of evil in the world is normally stated thus. If there is a god who is perfectly good, He must want to abolish evil; if He has unlimited power, He must be able to abolish evil. But evil exists, therefore, either God is not perfectly good or he is not unlimited power.

There are many forms of evil – natural, pain, moral and so forth – but for the purpose of this book we will discuss moral evil, since other evils, with the exclusion of natural disasters, (i.e. earthquake) spring directly or indirectly from moral evil. The problem of evil has been the topic of debate for many centuries, from Augustine to Leibniz, Tennant, John Hick, and Antony Flew. It is not the purpose here to give account of the arguments of various people but simply to note that attempts have been made over the Christian centuries to expound a Christian solution to the problem. The name for the attempted solution is 'theodicy' (its invention is attributed to Leibniz). Although more than one solution can be given to the problem, I suggest that the Christian hope for life after death is a very real solution to the theodicy and perhaps the only real solution to the 'theodicy' and perhaps the only real answer to human suffering and misery.

Moral evil is regarded as a wrong relationship to God, a turning away from God's will and turning towards self, self-interest, self-centeredness, instead of Christ-centeredness. In answering the question 'What is a right relation to God?' John Hicks states,

> The ideal relationship with God would consist of a vivid awareness of Him, at once joyous and awesome, and a whole-hearted worship of the infinite goodness and live by obedient self-sacrifice and love by obedient service to His presupposes within the creaturely realm. To know the creature centre of reality as personal active agape would be to accept gladly one's own status as a creature, utterly insignificant and yet loved and valued in God's free Grace, within a universe that wholly depends upon this activity.[45]

Hick goes on to stress that such knowledge relieves us from self-dependence; since we would look outside ourselves for comfort and support, God and not self would then be at the centre of our lives. We would then see others as children of God, and no longer envy, hatred, cruelty, and so forth, would be possible. We would realise that God loves one only as He loves all, with a caring, steadfast love that lasts forever.

Only one Person has lived a life of perfect obedience to God – His Only Son Jesus Christ. As stated earlier, it is only in Jesus that we see humanity as it is meant to be. All others, even the most saintly,

---

[45] John Hicks, 'Evil and the God of Love'.

have self-centredness to some degree, and the greatest cause of man's suffering has always been the self-centredness of man. To the above statements the sceptic would ask, 'Why then did God not create man in such a way that he would always be God-centred?' To reply to that question, we must ask another. 'Why did God create man?' God created man for eternal loving fellowship with Him. Love can never be one-sided. Man must respond to the love given by God with love. It is clear from the evidence of human relationships that love cannot be demanded from a person; a person can be forced to do many things, but love is not one of these things. Therefore, God created man as persons with limited free choice, as mentioned in the section on morality. Man is free to move towards or away from the Divine. Still the sceptic would persist, but his question would now be, 'Why then did God not make man in such a way that he would always choose the good and the right?'

In reply, we must point out that human freedom must be complete freedom. Each person is capable of the knowledge of God's will, of moral growth, forgiveness, and love, thus each person is responsible (morally) for his own actions or lack of actions. This life is indeed a time of soul-building (as stated earlier), and the process requires courage of one's convictions, honesty, physical courage, goodness, love and so forth. If man always chose the right and good because his freedom was manipulated, like a puppet on a string, even if that be a divine string, then there would be no need for values and value judgements in the world, since nobody would ever choose to do wrong.

I will not enter into the challenge of the free will defence made by Flew and J. K. Mackie. It will suffice to note that it has been taken seriously and attempts have been made to reply to this. However, with reference to Flew's hypnotic suggestion, I can only repeat what I have already written: God cannot instil in a man a response of love and true commitment.

John Hick summarises the rebuttal of the Flew Mackie challenge as follows: 'God can, without contradiction be conceived to have so constituted men that they would be guaranteed always freely to act rightly in relation to one another. But He cannot, without contradiction, be conceived to have so constituted men that they would be guaranteed freely, to respond to Himself in authentic faith, love and worship.'[46]

The freedom that man possesses contains a certain amount of unpredictability. We can never say (as before mentioned) how we will act in a given situation, nor can we know beforehand the results of our actions. We can pass judgement on the actions of others in any given situation. This exercise is difficult. Men, in their actions, are building or otherwise their personalities, and in the case of most moral people, they are responsible for their own actions; we can never see the whole picture either in others or in ourselves.

Dostoyevsky, in 'The Brothers Karamazov', sees deliberate cruelty as the greatest form of evil, and most people would agree with him. He tells a story of a cruel general. A small child has thrown a stone and hurt the general's dog. The man kept the child in an outhouse overnight, then ordered him to be stripped naked and forced him to run. Then the general turned his hounds loose, and they tore the child to pieces before his mother's eyes. The point of relating the story here is this: Each person is precious in the eyes of God, and each person has value as a person. We are capable, by free decision, of moral and spiritual growth. Men are justified by a good by which they grow spiritually. This good is part of the individual, and this exercise is difficult. Goodness flows from the goodness of God; individual human goodness is that by which man is justified. Thus any justification of human suffering must postulate life after death; otherwise, there is no justification for the child or his mother.

---

[46] Flew Mackie, 'The Freedom of Man'.

It was mentioned earlier that we cannot pass judgements on others' actions at a particular time. John Hick makes this point when he states that we are all capable of forgiving others, and then goes on to say that the general in the story may have lived the rest of his life in a saintly fashion. Who are we to forgive or judge – the wicked general or the saintly old gentleman? We are finite and fallible; we cannot see the whole picture, and our 'vision' is limited. How are we able to forgive at all? The answer is, because we have been forgiven. By the Incarnation, Cross, and Resurrection of Jesus, God has shown us that we are forgiven; by those same events we are judged. God says 'no', no moral evil, and by these same events we are given freedom. Christ's invitation, 'Come unto me all ye that are heavily laden . . .' is a gracious invitation, not a command.

Christians do believe that God is perfect goodness, He does not wish evil, but He has created creatures who can discern between right and wrong. God is all-powerful, the Creator of all there is, but His power is the power of love and never a dictatorship. It must be pointed out that the problem of evil becomes a problem by failing to take into account the whole of the Christian faith. Christianity has always been a faith of hope. We hope for and believe in another existence – life after death. This belief is the most sure, and I am convinced of the essential Christian standpoint in solving the 'theodicy'. No Christian would ever claim to know everything about the nature of God – God's nature is still a mystery and beyond the full understanding of a finite mind, as is God's scheme of things.

1 John Hicks, 'Evil and the God of Love'
2 Flew Mackie, 'The Freedom of Man'

CHAPTER 17

The Significance of Belief in Life after Death

In past centuries and at the present time, Christians have been criticised for their 'otherworldliness'. It is said that the Christian faith leads to a hope for life after death, which in turn leads to a negative attitude to this world. If this criticism is true, then, as Karl Marx said, 'religion is the opium of the people'. And we are living in an 'otherworldliness', which influences our attitude to this world and its problems. However, people who posit this argument need only to read history books to learn that many of the great social reforms have sprung out of Christian faith – for example, abolition of slavery, education of children of working-class parents, to mention two examples, but many more could be cited. John Baillie states the significance of Christian belief in life after death:

> If our hope in a fuller life beyond is to be recognised as a fine and manly thing, it must never lead us to be unjust to the values and the demands of the life that now is. It must never lessen our interest in the present life or make us feel it to be less worth living, or tempt us to hurry

> through it. It must never have the effect of taking our minds off our present tasks, so that that shall be done less thoroughly and well; rather is should lead to their more thorough and conscientious performance.[47]

It is true that in the Primitive Church there was no outcry against social injustice (i.e. slavery). Saint Paul's letter to the Corinthians bears witness to this. But it must be remembered that these early Christians thought that the 'end time' was imminent. It was only when the realisation dawned upon Christianity that the 'last days' were not imminent that Christendom began a movement for the reorganisation of society according to the rules of the brotherhood of man – a movement that was continued down through the centuries to the present time. This movement cannot be considered as an innovation, superimposed upon the faith by believers who suddenly realised that the 'end time' would not happen in their lifetime. The ideals of Christian brotherhood are grounded in Christ Himself in whom there is no Jew or Gentile, black or white. The atoning work of Christ is for all men everywhere. The two great commands, mentioned earlier, 'Love God with all your heart and all your soul and your neighbour as yourself' in the Person of Christ, and in these two great commands lies the 'foundation' for the concept of the brotherhood of man. As Emil Brunner wrote in *Man in Revolt*, 'our spiritual life participates both in the eternity of truth and the transitoriness of creaturely existence'.[48]There is no 'opting out' of this life with all its problems for the Christian. Even if he believes this life is not all and that he is not a self-dependent person but depends upon his Master for

---

[47] John Baillie, 'And the Lifer Everlasting'.

[48] E Brunner, 'Man in Revolt'.

all, the works and words of Jesus make it clear that we all have responsibility to other children of God.

Present generations are not less interested in a 'future' life than past generations were. In the past, both out with and within the Church, the belief was a point of mutual agreement. In the present, the reverse is too often the case. In the past, this life gained its significance from the fact that it was accepted as a pilgrimage to a better life. The present scepticism to the belief leads to a careless attitude to morals. If this life is all there is, why bother with the difference between right and wrong? Why not adopt the attitude of 'eat, drink and be merry for tomorrow we die'?

As mentioned earlier, the Christian does not strive for goodness because he wants to use it as a currency for entry into another existence after death. He does so because his goodness is truly good and is a step nearer the perfection that is revealed in his Master. He well knows that he cannot achieve that perfection but believes that in the life to come his goodness will have a chance of becoming more perfect.

Fosdick quotes Professor Hyslop, who stated, 'The ideals of democracy will live or die with the belief in immortality'.[49] In other words, it is the permanence of moral ideals that constitutes all that democracy stands for. To this, the humanist would argue that he will die, but his ideals will be carried. If there is no personal vindication for all the suffering in this world, especially when the innocent are the sufferers, as is often the case in future, then there is no hope for human freedom, because a person is never so free than when he realises that this temporal life is not all there is. With this kind of freedom come the courage, obligation, and commitment to stand by ideals of goodness, beauty, love, and so forth . . ., even when the 'odds' are very much against a person.

---

[49] Fosdick, 'The Assurance of Immortality'.

In this age we live in, people live in fear – not the anxiety and fear Heidegger speaks of but a fear that is much wider and deeper than past generations has ever known. We live in fear of nuclear, chemical, and viral warfare – the obliteration of the race on one side, and on the other side, there is fear of the society in which we live, whether this is a small unit of family of the large unit of nation on the other side. To the humanist we say, 'Look around you – the high ideals of past generations are not being upheld by a vast majority of young and old today.' Where now lie the humanist hope for future generations? His ideals are being distorted, at most forgotten altogether. It must be remembered that the Christ Himself was not vindicated this side of the grave. Jesus did not say, 'I die but my ideals live on.' He trusted in God's grace, and He shattered the power of death over His Father's children. He still lives on to show us the way to go. At this point I could do nothing better than to quote Fosdick with whom I am in full agreement and whose words I cannot improve upon:

> Justice cannot be preserved in a universe which does not preserve its moral gains. Without immortality society itself has a limited existence; since if a man believes that this life is all, then he will not seek reforms, but rather seek the best and most comfortable way he can find to journey through this life . . . The infinite value of personality which immortality asserts makes any fight for social justice worthwhile . . . Moral strivings are aimed at the building up or enriching or personal character, and personal character is the one means by which the universe may preserve its moral gains.[50]

50 Fosdick, 'The Assurance of Immortality'.

The Christian who accepts belief in eternal life not only hopes for this life in the future but also he lives eternal life in the here and now, because he lives the kind of life he would want to live for all eternity in the presence of his Master now and hereafter, in communion with God and his fellow men. His participation in a fellowship of love, both divine and human, is a foretaste of an even more beautiful fellowship of love in the life to come.

It must be noted that belief in life after death does not provide the believer with an unnatural attitude to death itself. Oscar Cullman made this point most clearly when he contrasted the sublime attitude to death that Socrates held; with the death of Christ with all its terror and pain. There is no Platonic dualism in Christian hope. We know that we will truly die, every part of us will die, and no part of us is either divine or immortal. However, by the grace of God, death will not hold us; the grave 'has lost its sting'.[51]That which will rise to live on in another existence is the whole of us, not as we are now but in some way like Jesus when He rose; the same yet different, what Saint Paul calls a spiritual body – different and yet the same personality.

For the Christian there is no unnatural longing for death; if this were so, we would have mass suicide. Death is still a natural fear, either the death of a loved one or one's own death. *We* cannot put into words what lies ahead any more than anybody can tell the unborn babe that he is entering a freer and more beautiful life. The hereafter is a mystery, but we have the comforting words of Christ Jesus: 'I go to prepare a place for you.'

51 'Man in Revolt', p. 470.

References

1. John Baillie, 'And the Lifer Everlasting'
2. E Brunner, 'Man in Revolt'
3. Fosdick, 'The Assurance of Immortality'
4. 'Man in Revolt', p. 470

BIBLIOGRAPHY

Aquinas St T. Summa contra Gentiles. English Translated by Fathers of the English Dominical Province in 22 vols. London 1964.

Aquinas St T. Summa Theologica. English Translated by The English Dominican Province in 22 vols. 2nd revised edition London, 1921–32. (Translated as Summa Theologica).

Augustine St City of God (T&T Clark, Edinburgh, 1971, and Random House, New York, 1950).

Baillie, J. and The *Life Everlasting* (Oxford University Press).

Brunner E. *Man in Revolt.* Translated by Olive Wyon (Lutterworth Press, London and Red Hill).

Brunner E. *The Divine Imperative.* Translated by Olive Wyon (Lutterworth Press, London and Redshill).

Copleston, F. Aquinas Harmondsworth (1955, reprinted 1970).

Copleston F. *History of Philosophy* (New York, 1962).

Crew F.A. 'The Meaning of Death.' In the Humanist Outlook, edited by A.J. Ayre.

Dostoyevsky F. *The Brothers Karamazov.* Heinemann, London 1912 and The Modern Library, New York, 1950.

Fosdick, H.E. The Assurance of Immortality (SCM Press).

Fraser Sir James Beliefin Immortality and Worship [of the Dead], vol. 1.

Heidegger. M. Existence and Being. Intro. by Werner Brook (Vision Press Ltd, London).

Hick J. *Evil and the God of Love* (The Fontana Library of Theology and philosophy 5th. ed., 1977).

Hick J. *Death and Eternal Life* (Colins, 1976).

Jowett B. *The Dialogues of Plato.* Translated. To English with Analyses and Introduction, vol. II, 3rd ed. (Oxford University Press).

Kant, I. Critique of Practical Reason Trans. Edited by Lewis White Beck (University of Chicago Press, 1949).

Korner, S. Kant (Penguin Books).

Lewis C.S. *The Great Divorce* (Collins Fontana Books).

Lewis H.D. *The Self and Immortality* (Macmillan).

Owen H.P. *The Moral Argument for Christian Theism* (George Allen and Unwin Ltd, 1965).

Phillips D.Z. *Death and Immortality* (Macmillan, London, and St. Martins Press, New York 1970).

Popper K. and Eccles, J.C. *The Self and Its Brain.*

Pringle-Pattison, A.E. *The Idea of Immortality* (Oxford Clarendon Press, 1922).

Ramsay Ian T. *Freedom and Immortality* (SCM Press).

Russell B. *Mysticism and Logic* (Longmans, Green, London, 1918).

Salmon S.D.F. *The Christian Doctrine of Immortality* (Edinburgh T& T. Clark, 1901) 4th ed.

Sartre J. P.

Smart M. *Historical Sections in the Philosophy of Religion* (SCM Press).

Swinburne R. *The Existence of God* (Clarendon Press).

Taylor A.E. *The Christian Hope of Immortality* (John Heritage) The Unicorn Press, London.

Taylor A.E. Plato, *The Man and His Work* (Macmillan & Co, Ltd. London 2nd ed.

Tillich, P., *Systematic Theology.* Vol. III (University of Chicago Press, Chicago, 1963 & Nesbit, London, 1964).

Holy Bible – RSV & AV.

CPSIA information can be obtained
at www.ICGtesting.com
Printed in the USA
FFOW04n1121050217
32093FF